Can You
Run the
Economy?

Can You Run the Economy?

JOE MAYES

EBURY
PRESS

1

Ebury Press, an imprint of Ebury Publishing
Penguin Random House UK
One Embassy Gardens, 8 Viaduct Gdns,
Nine Elms, London SW11 7BW

Ebury Press is part of the Penguin Random House group of companies
whose addresses can be found at global.penguinrandomhouse.com

First published by Ebury Press in 2025

www.penguin.co.uk

A CIP catalogue record for this book is available from the British Library

ISBN 9781529960716

Printed and bound in Great Britain by Clays Ltd, Elcograf S.p.A.

The authorised representative in the EEA is Penguin Random House Ireland,
Morrison Chambers, 32 Nassau Street, Dublin D02 YH68

Penguin Random House is committed to a sustainable future
for our business, our readers and our planet. This book is
made from Forest Stewardship Council® certified paper.

For Catherine and Madeleine

Contents

APPENDICES

Introduction

Congratulations! By opening this book, you've become one of the most powerful people in Britain. You're going to play the role of the Chancellor of the Exchequer – master of the nation's finances – in a government fast approaching a general election. Many historic figures have gone before you – William Gladstone, Benjamin Disraeli, David Lloyd George, Winston Churchill, Neville Chamberlain – to pick just a few. And now the latest name on that august roll call is yours.

The stakes are high. You're taking the controls of one of the world's biggest economies, the prosperity of 68 million people in your hands. One misstep could crash both financial markets and your political career. Every word you say will be scrutinised. Every business lobbyist in the country wants your ear. But play your cards right and you'll make the country a wealthier and happier place. You'll also be in pole position to be the next prime minister.

The journey ahead will be filled with dilemmas and tough choices. You'll learn all there is to know about leading an advanced economy, all while managing the pressures and pitfalls of democracy. Luckily, you'll have the best advisors to help you: chancellors who've filled your shoes, no less. Norman Lamont, Philip Hammond, Kwasi Kwarteng, Jeremy Hunt, Rachel Reeves ... their words of wisdom will guide you.

And just like them, you'll face two major pressures. The first is your – and by extension, your government's – popularity. You serve only at the pleasure of the voters, and they'll turf you out if you don't keep them on side. The decisions you make as chancellor will affect your party's poll ratings and its chances of winning the upcoming election. Don't be surprised if the prime minister fires you should the public turn against you.

The second is the health of the government's finances. Your resources are finite and you'll have to make wise, prudent choices in testing circumstances. Yes, you need to curry favour with the voters, but you also face stark economic limits that constrain your action. Spend too much or be too careless and you'll risk the wrath of financial markets. And remember: triggering a market meltdown is also certain to cost you your job.

So, as you embark on your journey as chancellor, have pen or pencil handy and keep note of two things on your tracker on p. 4. The first is your **approval rating**. Your aim is to keep this as high as possible, to give yourself the best chance of winning the election. The good news is you begin with a net score of **+10**. Voters have taken a liking to you in your political career so far and are eager to see you deliver results. But if your poll rating drops too low, beware. Politics is a very dangerous place for the unpopular.

The second is your **budget surplus**. This is the amount of money you have for spending. You'll want to save most of it for your big, set-piece moment – the Budget – but it'll also be there for the various emergencies and surprises that are an inevitable feature of politics. You begin with a surplus of **£20 billion**. That might sound like a lot, but it's a mere 1.6 per cent of the £1.2 trillion that the government spends each year, a fragile starting point in these uncertain economic times. So again, beware. If your surplus gets too low, investors will start to get jittery and you could lose control of the economy.

That's enough by way of a preamble. A new dawn is breaking over Westminster and your work as chancellor is about to begin. So, are you ready?

TRACKER

Budget Surplus	Approval Rating
£ 20 billion	+10
£	
£	
£	
£	
£	
£	
£	
£	
£	
£	
£	
£	
£	
£	
£	
£	
£	
£	

PART 1

Starting at No. 11 Downing Street

Apart from being prime minister,
there is no better job.

Jeremy Hunt, Chancellor of the Exchequer, 2022–4

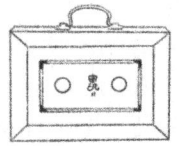

CHAPTER 1

Decisions, Decisions

You feel a very heavy responsibility.
Norman Lamont, Chancellor of the Exchequer, 1990–3

You walk into the Treasury – the majestic white complex at 1 Horse Guards on Whitehall, with the royal residence of Buckingham Palace radiant opposite across the quaint ponds of St James's Park – and are met with a sea of applause and smiling faces.

'Congratulations, chancellor,' successive bright-eyed officials say with vigorous handshakes, as you're led to your new office and presented with the famous red ministerial briefcase, the gold letters of 'Chancellor of the Exchequer' glinting. It all feels like a whirlwind. Just hours earlier, you were a mere junior minister, a rising star of British politics on the cusp of your big break. And then the surreal blur: a phone call from the prime minister herself, the famous walk up the cobbles to 10 Downing Street, the click-click-click of camera shutters, the simple invitation – 'I'd like you to be my chancellor' – and then a short stroll over to the Treasury into a world of power. Deferential nods, looks of expectation, close protection officers and an army of civil servants at your beck and call. For today, at least, you're the hottest political name in Britain.

'Chancellor, if I may.'

Your day-dreaming admiration of your new red box is interrupted by the tall, kindly gentleman who'd first greeted you at the Treasury entrance. The stories about this bespectacled man are legendary: consigliere to chancellors down the decades, Sir Alex Davidson has seen and heard it all. Chief civil servant in the Treasury, also known as the permanent secretary, the twinkle in Sir Alex's eye is like that of a wise old teacher ready to instruct their latest pupil. He's in charge of enforcing all the decisions you're going to make. After you, he's the next most powerful person in the building.

'We'd normally run through the introductory briefings on a day like today,' Sir Alex says. 'But unfortunately there's a matter that requires your urgent attention. It's at the top of your box. The X-Tech case.'

You open the briefcase and see the memo marked CONFIDENTIAL, already anticipating its contents. You've been following this sorry saga in the newspapers: the impending collapse of a revolutionary green energy company that employs tens of thousands of people across Britain, scuttled by an internal accounting scandal and scrambling to survive. Their futile search for financial rescue has been going on for weeks, dominating the headlines.

'I'm afraid your predecessor hadn't decided whether the government should intervene,' Sir Alex says. 'The prime minister is wavering too. And time's up. If X-Tech can't raise the funds by this evening, it's over.'

You're just about to ask Sir Alex about the terms of any potential bailout when there's a knock at the door. In walks a lady whom you're very glad to see.

'Chancellor,' the woman says with a flourish and a bow. 'Sounds magnificent, doesn't it? I always knew you'd make it. What did I say when you were first elected? *Future prime minister*. And here we are. A stone's throw away.'

'Thank you, Polly,' you say.

This is Polly Tickle, all-round Westminster supremo and your long-time closest advisor and friend. At every significant moment in your career, she's been there: the welcoming head of your local party association who encouraged you to stand for elected office, the lady who then ran your campaign and hand-delivered umpteen fliers bearing your name and face, the woman who has become a household name in her own right as one of the canniest observers and operators in Whitehall. If you're ever in doubt about what will be best for your career – what will curry most favour with the prime minister, what will land best with the public, what might shift the polls in your favour – just ask Polly. She sees the X-Tech memo on your desk and nods.

'Ah yes,' she says. 'A poisoned chalice left by our dear departed chancellor. No wonder his heart gave out. But we have no choice. We have to save it, right?'

She looks between you and Sir Alex.

'Isn't it obvious?' Polly continues. 'All those job losses, this close to an election? And that be your *first* act as chancellor? Gives me the shivers.'

You spy the cost of the bailout on the memo and read it aloud. One billion pounds.

'And it'll be the best billion you ever spend,' Polly says.

There's a fresh knock at the door. Your heads turn and another person you're also very glad to see enters: the brilliant young economist, June Marion Keyes.

'Chancellor,' June says, bowing. 'Very sorry I'm late. Huge queue at security to get my pass. And then someone wanted a selfie. And then another person. And then another.'

You laugh. You're not the only well-known figure starting at the Treasury today: a darling of economics academia, June was your hire straight out of Oxford, one of the best decisions you ever made. Intellectually fearless and forthright with her views, June has an impeccable intuition on economics. She's also rather pugnacious and doesn't mince her words. She too sees the X-Tech memo.

'Of course,' June says. 'Well, at least your first decision is easy.'

She scans your face, frowns.

'Chancellor, surely you're not thinking of saving it? Bailing out that crooked executive team with hard-earned taxpayers' money and sending a message to all of corporate Britain that the government will pick up the bill whenever things go wrong? It's a terrible precedent. It'll just encourage excessive risk-taking in future, even more bad behaviour.'

June takes in the rest of the room, clocks Polly's squint.

'I think you're forgetting the human cost,' Polly says.

'I'm not,' June says. 'People will lose their jobs, yes. But they'll find new ones. It's called the labour market. I'm sorry, chancellor, but I think this is actually rather straightforward. The government really shouldn't be getting involved here.'

You look between Polly and June. An uncomfortable silence descends.

Eventually, Sir Alex says: 'It's a truism, chancellor, but no less true for it. Advisors advise and ministers decide. And you are now the minister. I must insist on an answer tonight.'

You take an inward breath and pick up your pen, hand hovering over the memo. It's time to make your first decision.

DECISION

Save the company. You agree with Polly. You want to make a strong first impression with the public and that calls for a bold intervention. You also want to send a signal to international investors that the UK is a good place to deploy their money, and the government will be there to help in difficult times. *Deduct £1 billion from your surplus.* If you choose this option, turn to p. 12.

Let the company go bust. You agree with June. It shouldn't fall on the hard-working taxpayer to bail out wealthy executives when they've made a mess. You want to convey an image of a strong chancellor who's willing to make the tough decisions in the interests of the public finances. *No cost.* If you choose this option, turn to p. 14.

OFFICIAL – SENSITIVE

YOU SAVE THE COMPANY

'Sometimes the politics has to come first, expensive as this may be,' you say, agreeing with Polly.

June frowns but she's a professional and immediately supports your decision.

'Certainly, chancellor,' she says.

'Excellent,' Sir Alex says. 'We'll arrange a statement for the markets and organise the announcement for tomorrow. Thank you for your decisiveness.'

You're reminding yourself of the terms of the bailout the following morning – the number of seats the government will take on X-Tech's board, the assurances that jobs will be retained, the share of future company profits that will flow to the taxpayer – when Polly leans over, speaking over the hum of your ministerial black Jaguar en route to X-Tech's headquarters.

'The PM is obviously delighted,' she says. 'I think the media are on our side too. *The people's chancellor.* That's what I've been telling journalists. Always looking out for the working man and woman. Champion of British business.'

She reaches under her passenger seat, unfurling a yellow hard hat and high-viz jacket.

'Remember,' she says. 'Wear these. It'll look great. Trust me.'

Polly is proved correct. The evening news leads on you announcing the rescue – a group of relieved employees at your shoulder, the hard hat conveying an image of a chancellor getting stuck in on the economy – and the country's political commentators give you the thumbs-up. You've averted joblessness for tens of thousands of worried people as a general election fast approaches. With any luck, they'll remember your generosity on voting day. There are some naysayers, naturally – June's argument about rewarding recklessness is repeated in the right-wing press, and some say the £1 billion might've been better spent on schools and hospitals – but, on balance, the consensus is positive.

'And look at that,' Polly says via message, sending you a snap poll before you go to bed. 'An immediate bump. What did I say? *Future prime minister.*'

Add two points to your approval rating.
Now turn to p. 16.

YOU LET THE COMPANY GO BUST

You tell Polly that you get the politics but you think June is right. 'And it's a huge sum of money,' you say. 'We'll find better ways we can spend this.'

Polly can't mask a flicker of disappointment, but she manages a brave face.

'If you're sure, chancellor,' she says. 'I'll tell No. 10.'

Sir Alex claps his hands together and says, 'Very good. We'll communicate this to the company. And we'll ensure any affected workers are informed about government support for finding new employment. Thank you for your decisiveness.'

The next 48 hours are rather uncomfortable. Britain's media comes out against your decision, blaming you personally for the sudden wave of redundancies and calling it a grave mistake. '*Britain's absent chancellor,*' the *Times* leader column declares. '*Already missing in action,*' says the *Guardian*. '*What message does this send about Britain's openness for business?*' asks the *Independent*. A few minority voices in the right-wing press congratulate you for letting capitalism take its course, arguing that the company's collapse will see workers and investment redistributed to more productive firms, and that taxpayers' money has wisely been kept in the Treasury coffers. But that angle is largely drowned out by the negativity.

Your unease deepens when Polly, who's been subdued since your decision and clearly desperate to say 'I told you so', slips you a chart showing an immediate hit to your poll ratings.

'Just an early blip,' she says, her enthusiasm strained. 'Nothing we can't bounce back from.'

You're gloomily studying the polling numbers when June sees you and says: 'You did the right thing, chancellor. I know it doesn't win you many plaudits in the short term, but we need to protect our position ahead of the Budget. This was a victory for sound economics. You'll be more than vindicated in time. Trust me.'

Deduct three points from your political approval rating.
Now turn to p. 16.

CHAPTER 2

The Exchequer

*The Treasury has a small number
of people, but a lot of power.*
Philip Hammond, Chancellor of the Exchequer, 2016–19

You arrive at the Treasury the next morning still reeling from the sudden burden of responsibility and influence that comes with the role. Sir Alex is already waiting and appears to read your thoughts.

'They don't call it a Great Office of State for nothing,' Sir Alex says, inviting you to join him on a walkabout. 'I'm afraid the decisions will come thick and fast.'

The Treasury that Sir Alex shows you lacks the grandeur of the Foreign Office across the road – where the internal opulence and royal portraits are designed to impress overseas dignitaries – but it's nevertheless a bright, buzzing department, off-shooting rooms filled with headset-wearing officials tapping away at their desks. He enjoys regaling you at various points of interest: here the Churchill Room with its blue marble, where the former prime minister addressed the crowds from the balcony on VE Day in 1945 and ex-chancellor Gordon Brown announced the Bank of England's independence in 1997; there the unusual circular courtyard known as the 'drum', inspired by the designs of Italian Renaissance architect Andrea Palladio; here the chancellor's old office, once Bomber Command during the war. He's pointing out the site of a former machine gun post looking over St James's Park when you gasp. You've almost tripped over a black cat.

'The silent assassin,' Sir Alex says, chuckling. 'Meet Gladstone. Named after one of your most famous predecessors. Our rather prolific mouser-in-chief.'

Gladstone takes you in. He looks to Sir Alex and meows.

'Yes,' Sir Alex says. 'You've outlived yet another one.'

Sir Alex's tour becomes more business-like as you meet the key teams in the department, starting with the tax officials.

'Forgive me if this is all terribly obvious,' Sir Alex says, removing his glasses and cleaning them with a pocket cloth. 'But I think it's always best to cover the fundamentals. You'd be surprised how little some of your predecessors knew about public finances and the economy.'

His gaze becomes distant and you sense a painful memory. But then his glasses are replaced and it passes.

'Taxation,' he says. 'Perhaps the most important thing we do here in the Treasury. The government raises almost £1 trillion in taxes each year, and all the key decisions are made in this building. By you. It's really quite breathtaking when you think about it. The sway you have over the finances of every citizen in the country. When they go to work, you decide what they pay in income tax. Whenever someone pays for a meal in a restaurant or buys something in a shop or goes to the cinema, you decide what they pay in VAT. Whenever someone buys a home, you decide what they pay in stamp duty. And so on.'

Sir Alex motions to an official, who nods and disappears.

'You'll learn that setting tax rates is both an art and a science,' Sir Alex says. 'Set the rates too high and you'll face a very unhappy Joe Public, aggrieved by the burden and perhaps encouraged to conceal their gains or diminish their efforts. But set them too low, and you won't be able to afford the public services Joe Public expects.'

The official returns, wheeling a whiteboard displaying a pie chart.

'Thank you,' Sir Alex says. 'This is worth studying. A breakdown of the taxation we raise.'

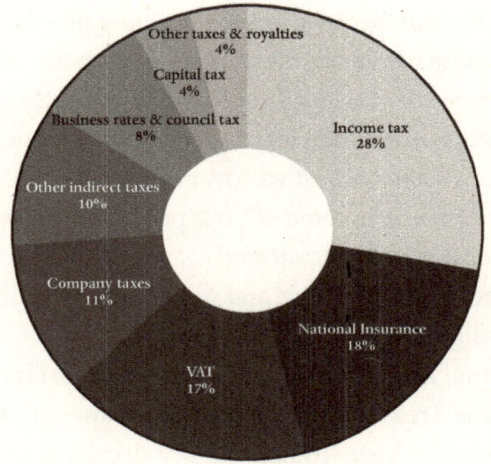

Where does the government get its money? | *Institute for Fiscal Studies*

'It's always helpful to know your golden geese, so to speak,' he says. 'As you can see, it's income tax, VAT, National Insurance and company taxes that are our biggest revenue-raisers. I'm sure we'll discuss these in greater detail ahead of the Budget.'

Your tour continues. You arrive at the Public Spending teams where the officials appear to be poring over umpteen complex spreadsheets.

'And this is what it's all for,' Sir Alex says, gesturing grandly. 'These fine folk finance 45 per cent of the UK economy. More than £1 trillion of spending.'

A few of the civil servants look up, embarrassed. One waves.

'This is the engine room of the British government,' Sir Alex says. 'Whenever anyone interacts with the state – an operation in the NHS, say, or receiving their benefits, or sending their child to the local comprehensive – that can only happen because the money was first made available here. Take our brave Armed Forces stationed overseas. Or our nuclear submarines patrolling the darkest waters of the ocean, keeping Britain safe. Or our spies working undercover in hostile regimes. The list goes on and on. The entire breadth and depth of government activity funded from here.'

More awkward acknowledgements. Sir Alex asks if they have the chart and another whiteboard materialises.

'Again, a breakdown for you,' he says. 'This is where the money goes.'

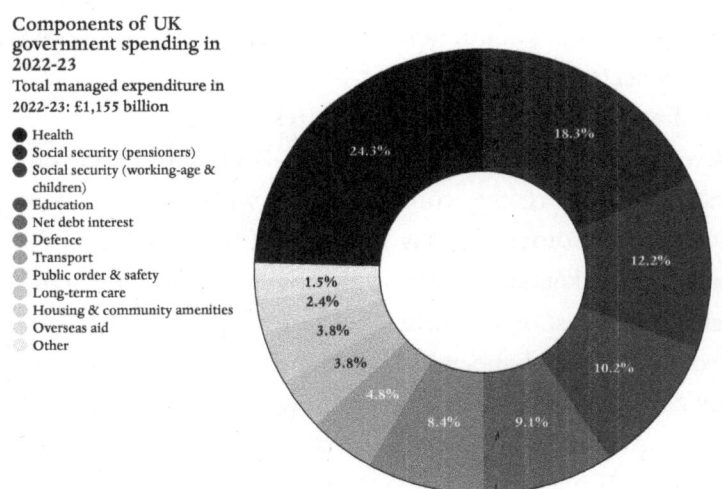

Components of UK government spending in 2022-23
Total managed expenditure in 2022-23: £1,155 billion

- Health
- Social security (pensioners)
- Social security (working-age & children)
- Education
- Net debt interest
- Defence
- Transport
- Public order & safety
- Long-term care
- Housing & community amenities
- Overseas aid
- Other

What does the government spend money on? | *Institute for Fiscal Studies*

'As you can see, the National Health Service, welfare and education are the biggest areas of spending.'

You consider the chart closely. You note that spending on debt interest is almost double the spending on defence, a point you mention to Sir Alex.

'An astute observation,' he says. 'And that's why I'd like you to meet these people.'

You come to your final stop on the tour: the Debt and Reserves Management (DRM) team. Sir Alex explains that the government doesn't only raise money through taxation. It also borrows money on financial markets and does so to plug any gaps between the money raised in tax and the money spent on public services.

'Hence we have government debt,' he says. 'Rather a lot of it, in fact. And of course, we pay interest on that debt. That's money we could be spending on schools, roads and hospitals, but, alas, we must pay our way with our creditors. They include pension funds, foreign investors and the like.'

Sir Alex looks about himself, lowers his voice. He beckons you closer.

'I wanted to bring you here to stress a singular point. You never want to hear from these people. Ever. If you find yourself on an emergency conference call with someone from DRM, then something has gone badly wrong. You see, if financial markets suddenly start demanding higher and higher rates of interest on our debt – because they lose faith in you, and I've seen this happen before – then our economic position can collapse rather quickly. Something to bear in mind.'

Sir Alex pulls away and is jovial again, leading you back to your office. He wishes you the best of luck in the role and asks what's next on your agenda.

'A meeting with leaders from two of Britain's largest trade unions,' you say.

Sir Alex's face falls.

'Then luck is certainly what you will need,' he says.

Polly and your diary manager are in your office moments later, announcing that the union bosses have arrived. Polly's face is a picture of alarm.

'Just to warn you, chancellor,' she says. 'Be prepared. I've seen some scary people in my time. But not quite as scary as this.'

You settle yourself at your desk. 'Send them in,' you say.

CHAPTER 3

Industrial Relations

You can't say yes to everything.
Rachel Reeves, Chancellor of the Exchequer, 2024–

The two men – Charlie Marks and Fred Angel – take seats across from you. Between them they represent the overwhelming majority of Britain's unionised public sector workforce of doctors, nurses, train drivers, bus drivers, civil servants, firefighters, police, teachers, and so on. They get straight to the point.

'We appreciate you're new here, chancellor,' Marks says, as he massages his knuckles. 'And the pay deal was obviously drawn up by your predecessor, so we don't hold that against you. But surely you see this for what it is. An *insulting* offer.'

On the desk between you, flecked with the saliva from Marks's 'insulting', is a summary of what he's referring to: the Treasury's proposed public sector pay offer. One of your biggest decisions each year – covering more than 20 per cent of government spending and affecting 6 million workers – the previous chancellor had pencilled in a 5 per cent pay rise, in line with the recommendation of the independent pay review bodies. They're the panels of experts who advise on the settlement, bringing an impartiality to the decision which is meant to dissipate the tension of confrontations like these.

'Only 5 per cent,' Angel chips in, also moistening your ministerial memo. 'At a time when inflation is already running at 5 per cent?'

His tone becomes funereal.

'What a slap in the face for our hard-working members. For the people who are the backbone of Britain.'

You say you hear their concerns and you're sympathetic, but you remind them that the public finances are already tight and you're simply following the independent recommendations.

'Chancellor, you might think we've come here to negotiate,' Marks says, cracking a forefinger. 'Well, you'd be wrong. We're long since done negotiating with this government. The excuses have worn thin. We've come to tell you what you're going to do. You will award all public sector workers a 10 per cent pay rise immediately, without caveat or qualification. If not, you will face a general strike.'

He says those last two words with menace befitting the threat. It paints a picture in your mind of rubbish piling high in the streets; of parents at a loss for childcare because of the closure of their kids' schools; of many more deaths in the NHS due to patients not receiving treatment; of lengthening backlogs in the courts and crimes going unpunished; of mass disruption on the railways, buses and underground services, leaving people unable to get to work; of production in factories grinding to a halt; the huge negative economic and political impact of all of the above, and more. Strikes in individual public sectors are painful enough, but this is the nuclear option.

'Yes, chancellor,' Marks whispers, reading your face. 'A *general* strike.'

You take a moment to gather yourself once the pair have left, surprised by the brevity of the meeting and rattled by the extremity of their demand. Polly and June join you for a much-needed restorative sugary doughnut and strong coffee in the Treasury's cafe downstairs, where you fill them in on the ultimatum. Polly is aghast.

'You know the worst thing?' she says. 'They've got us over a barrel. And they know it. That kind of disruption is terminal in an election year. It will ruin us. It will ruin you, chancellor. We have to accept their terms.'

June says she strongly disagrees. She says the pay demands are dangerous, unaffordable and will stoke inflation. Polly asks why.

'Because it's a huge extra injection of cash into the economy that won't be matched by an increase in the amount of *stuff* in the economy – the goods people buy,' June says. 'So it's just more money chasing the same amount of goods. Companies will realise this and increase prices, seeing a chance to boost profits. And they'll definitely increase prices if their own employees also start pushing for 10 per cent pay rises, as they will. Then we risk a vicious cycle. The trade unions will be back next year asking for even more money, to compensate their members for everything being even more expensive. And then we'll be in a wage–price spiral. Rising inflation, rising wage demands, and it's a feedback loop.'

Polly is still sceptical, dangling her pastry with a frown.

'I say keep it simple,' Polly says. 'We can put significant money directly into the pockets of many voters, all while avoiding these strikes. And those strikes would be bad for the economy anyway, wouldn't they?'

Your ministerial briefing note on the matter of public sector pay and industrial action had also made this point.

Depending on their length, disruption from strikes can cost the economy billions of pounds in lost output, a thought you mention now.

'We should still call their bluff,' June says. 'Reject their demands and call for further negotiations. I bet they'd settle for 7 per cent, or even 6 per cent. And if they strike, we say we're simply defending sound government finances, and any disruption is the fault of the unions alone. The strikers would eventually run out of money and public support. And, most importantly, we won't be fuelling the fire of inflation.'

You thank them both and return to your office, deciding there's one more opinion you'd like to seek: that of the prime minister herself. You get through to her on a secure line – she's currently on a diplomatic visit in the Middle East – though you sense she's rather distracted.

'I trust your judgement,' the PM says over the background hubbub of what sounds like a formal state dinner: chinking glasses, lively music, genteel chatter. Your mention of the alarming cost of what the unions are asking for – an extra £10 billion spent on public sector pay – appears not to have registered.

'That's why I picked you as my chancellor, after all,' she says. 'I'm sure you'll make the right call.'

You hang up with feigned confidence and return to your ministerial box. It's time to make your next decision.

DECISION

Accept the 10 per cent pay rise. You think Polly is right. What better way to win public support than just giving more money to voters? You're also worried about the threat of these strikes. You hear June's concerns about inflation but an election is looming, and that can be a worry for another day. *Deduct £10 billion from your surplus.* If you choose this option, turn to p. 28.

OFFICIAL – SENSITIVE

DECISION

Reject the unions' demand and call for further negotiations. You think June is right. You want to keep a lid on price rises in the economy and also get the best value for money for the taxpayer. The threat of strikes is concerning, but you think you can get the unions to agree to less. No cost. If you choose this option, turn to p. 30.

YOU GIVE THE UNIONS
THE 10 PER CENT PAY RISE

You ask your principal private secretary to get Charlie Marks on the phone.

'That's a very wise move,' Marks says, on hearing your decision, his delight audible. 'Pleasure doing business with you, chancellor.'

June goes a shade paler when you break the news to her and Polly, but Polly is bouncing.

'Brilliant call, chancellor,' she says. 'I'll brief the papers now.'

She adopts her newsreader voice.

'Payday for Britain! Hard-working public servants finally get the pay rise they deserve. All thanks to their new, finger-on-the-pulse, champion-of-the-people, chancellor. The *Guardian* is going to love it. The *Mirror* too. The *Telegraph* will call us commies but *plus ça change.*'

'And I'll prepare a briefing on the likely response of the Bank of England,' June says darkly as she leaves, not looking you in the eye.

'Don't worry about her,' Polly says. 'Those economists. Too obsessed with the numbers. Never thinking about the politics.'

June re-enters, having overheard, and says: 'I'm always thinking about the politics. And just you watch. We'll pay a serious political price for this.'

Yet in the days that follow, there's no sign of June's prophecy coming true. A majority of Britain's newspapers report favourably on the pay deal, saying it will give a much-needed boost to morale in the UK public sector and marks a long-overdue recognition of their social contribution. A minority in the right-wing press attacks you for all the reasons raised by June – the potential for stoking inflation, the major hit to the public purse – but thankfully it's just that, a minority.

At the end of the week, Polly slaps a fresh polling chart on your desk, her expression smug.

'Power to the people,' she says.

Add one point to your approval rating.
Now turn to p. 32.

YOU REJECT THE UNIONS' DEMAND

'Turns out you weren't listening, chancellor,' Charlie Marks says over the phone, his voice bitter, laughing at your request for further talks. 'We've already had the talks! Don't bother coming back with anything other than 10 per cent. See you on the picket line.'

The disruption that follows is just as bad as you feared. By the second day, most schools in England are closed. On the third day, the NHS declares an emergency due to staff shortages. On the fourth day, Polly stops showing you the front pages of the newspapers, too depressed by what they contain, Britain's headline writers running out of synonyms for 'chaos' and 'crisis'. June was right about one thing – there's plenty of public anger at the unions themselves – but you're also getting lots of the blame.

'We just need to hold the line,' June says, sounding very unsure of herself. 'Surely they'll come back to the negotiating table.'

As it is, you never find out if they do. On the fifth day, with your latest offer of talks having just been rebuffed by the unions, you hear from the prime minister, who's calling from her Royal Air Force jet as she travels back from the Middle East.

'Chancellor, remember how I said I trust your judgement on this one,' she says, sounding the very opposite of distracted now. 'Well … I think we need to change course. Immediately.

This is hurting us too much. I want you to make the strikes stop. Right now.'

You feel deeply uneasy, winded by this direct attempt at an overrule by the prime minister. You consider arguing the case for staying the course – the inflationary impact, the hit to the public finances – but Polly is in your eyeline drawing an imaginary line across her throat, while June's gaze is downcast.

'Certainly, prime minister,' you say, feeling humiliated. 'We'll get this sorted.'

You invite Marks and Angel back into the Treasury for an emergency meeting and they enter with a swagger. You say you'd be willing to do 9 per cent, final offer. Marks shakes his head, says you're still not listening. They make to leave but then you finally concede: Fine. 10 per cent.

'You could've saved yourself a lot of pain here, chancellor,' Angel says, no doubt referring to the hit you've taken in the polls. 'Remember this for next time. We never make empty threats.'

Deduct £10 billion from your surplus and three points from your approval rating. Now turn to p. 32.

CHAPTER 4

Into No. 11

Living at No. 11 is something I never took for granted.
Alistair Darling, Chancellor of the Exchequer 2007–10

You're a fortnight into your time as chancellor when Sir Alex arrives early for a meeting with you in No. 11 Downing Street, your new residence and workplace which adjoins the most famous address in Britain. Chancellors typically split their time between the Treasury and No. 11 according to personal preference, and you've already taken a liking to the historic rooms of this quaint seventeenth-century Georgian house. Sir Alex is about to take a sip of his tea when he looks at you and your advisors with alarm.

'We haven't given you the full tour, have we?' he says. 'Let's rectify that immediately.'

Sir Alex leads you into the hallway, the first place you see when you enter the famous black door of No. 11. A small and modest space, with a Vulliamy grandfather clock and marble fireplace, it's dominated by two portraits of the nineteenth century's great political adversaries: William Gladstone and Benjamin Disraeli. Sir Alex explains that many see Gladstone, who was chancellor on four occasions between 1852 and

1882, as the grandfather of how the Treasury thinks about economics now. 'His beliefs in free trade, free markets and sound money remain key parts of the Treasury ethos today,' Sir Alex says.

'And he went on to be prime minister four times,' Sir Alex says, pointing to Gladstone's portrait. 'Disraeli managed the same feat twice.'

Polly's eyes widen in awe.

'Did you hear that, chancellor?' she says. 'Prime minister *four times*. No shame in dreaming big.'

You continue through the hallway and arrive at an inter-secting corridor. To your right is a door that leads directly into No. 10 Downing Street. To your left leads to No. 12 Downing Street, now used as the No. 10 press office. Sir Alex notes that, on occasions in history when there has been tension between the chancellor and prime minister, without naming any names, then the chancellor liked to keep the connecting door with No. 10 closed. 'Though I'm sure that won't be necessary this time around,' he says with a wink.

You cross the corridor and enter the sitting room of No. 11. Sir Alex explains that, in yesteryear, this room was used as the location for pre-recording the Budget Day broadcast, the chancellor's direct address to the nation that would go out on the evening of Budget Day. It also had to serve as a temporary holding pen for the poor unfortunate crew who recorded said broadcast, given they had advance knowledge of the Budget's contents and weren't allowed to leave Downing Street. Today, the Budget broadcasts are recorded in other parts of the house and the sitting room is used for informal meetings, while also hosting a few desks for the chancellor's private secretaries.

At the end of the sitting room, on the right, is what Sir Alex calls the most architecturally significant room in No.

11: the dining room. Designed by renowned eighteenth-century architect Sir John Soane, it has a magnificent vaulted ceiling and lightwells which allow daylight to fall on the long-panelled walls. This room is often used by the chancellor for meetings with captains of industry and finance, as well as being a favoured spot for Budget planning. Polly runs a finger approvingly along the smooth, varnished table.

Next, Sir Alex takes you into the No. 11 study, which is at the end of the sitting room, on the left. With two large windows looking out onto the Downing Street garden and its bookcases lined with red-bound copies of Hansard, recording years and years of historic Parliamentary debate, it's a cosy space, perfect for knuckling down to work and holding meetings with your closest aides and staff. A portrait of the chancellor's choosing typically hangs on the wall behind your desk, and Sir Alex says he looks forward to seeing whom you will select.

'Rishi Sunak and Jeremy Hunt chose a picture of Nigel Lawson, Margaret Thatcher's famous tax-cutting chancellor of the 1980s,' Sir Alex says. 'Rachel Reeves opted for Ellen Wilkinson, a radical figure of British socialism and feminism in the early twentieth century. The choice is yours.'

You return through the sitting room and head to the famous staircase of No. 11, which features portraits and caricatures of the chancellors who've gone before you. The first face at the bottom of the staircase is that of William Pitt the Younger, who served concurrently as prime minister and chancellor from 1783 to 1801, and then again from 1804 to 1806. Sir Alex notes that it was Pitt who first levied your biggest revenue-raiser: income tax, introduced in 1799 to fund the Napoleonic Wars.

'It was only meant to be a temporary measure,' Sir Alex says. 'Alas, look at all our payslips today.'

Sir Alex points out other names of interest – like George Ward Hunt, chancellor in 1868 under Disraeli, and also the nephew of the great-great-great grandfather of Jeremy Hunt, who became chancellor 154 years later. Towards the top of the staircase, you see the chancellors of the late twentieth and early twenty-first centuries depicted in political cartoons of their choosing. Among them, you spot Philip Hammond being eaten by a crocodile called 'Brexit', George Osborne being squashed by the 'elephant in the room' of government debt, and Gordon Brown handing out wads of cash to grateful public sector workers.

'One day your cartoon will hang here too,' Sir Alex says. 'May it depict prosperity and success.'

You've arrived at the final stop on the tour: the state drawing room on the first floor, which runs the entire width of No. 11. Sir Alex explains that this room is most regularly used for formal occasions, with notable features including two of No. 11's finest treasures – a pair of antique black and gold lacquered Chinese cabinets – and the grand eighteenth-century marble fireplaces at either end surrounded by ornate mirrors.

'You will host many an illustrious dignitary in here,' Sir Alex says, seating himself on one of the stately cream sofas. 'Far more illustrious than I. Though, while we're here, perhaps we could begin our meeting.'

You sit across from him with Polly and June and Sir Alex offers you a dossier.

'I understand you're speaking to a rather important person tomorrow,' Sir Alex says. 'Which is why I've prepared you this.'

CHAPTER 5

Meeting the Governor

*A well-functioning government will deliver
well-coordinated fiscal and monetary policy.*
Philip Hammond

You have Sir Alex's dossier open in your lap the next day as your ministerial Jaguar heads towards the Bank of England in the City, London's financial district. You're about to meet one of the most powerful figures in the British economy.

'So, what can we expect from our man the governor?' Polly asks, looking up out of the blacked-out windows and goggling at the skyscrapers of the Square Mile. The Bank – which Sir Alex's file helpfully reminds you has roles including managing the supply of cash in society and regulating high street banks and the financial system – also famously controls interest rates, and June repeats her prediction that the governor will want to raise rates to curb inflation. The Bank is mandated by the government to target an inflation rate of 2 per cent, and moves interest rates up and down to that end.

'It won't be a good look,' June says. 'It'll be monetary policy – what the Bank does – and fiscal policy – what we do in terms of tax and spend – moving in opposite directions.'

Polly says she's never quite understood why everyone gets so bothered about that inflation malarky anyway. You sense from her sideways smirk that she's winding June up. June takes the bait. 'Inflation is a goldilocks concept,' she says. 'We want neither too little nor too much of it. Too little inflation – indeed, deflation, where prices are falling – makes people defer spending because goods will be cheaper in future. And because they're not spending and there's less demand for stuff, prices keep falling. All the while companies are laying off staff because they're not selling goods. And then it's a downward spiral. But too much inflation is also a problem,' she says. 'Imagine if prices were going up 10 per cent a year, or even 15 per cent or 20 per cent. Your savings would quickly lose their value. People who get by on fixed payments – like pensioners, or those on welfare – would find themselves able to buy less and less. We'd all get poorer, and fast. So, we want a little bit of inflation, but not too much.'

'Got it,' Polly says, pleading forgiveness for her rusty economics. 'I'll go back to reading Sir Alex's file.'

You arrive at Threadneedle Street and Polly reacts to your tour of the Bank with a succession of whistles: at the vaults of gold, the pretty Garden Court with its mulberry trees, the cantilever staircase overlooking an original Roman mosaic. She declares that the Treasury is a paupers' dive in comparison; June points out that the Bank has rather a lot more money. Your meeting with the governor then begins cordially enough, but the atmosphere changes when you come to inflation.

'Chancellor, you're well aware that inflation is currently above target,' he says, referring to the 5 per cent rate. 'We'd been making good progress addressing the situation. But your pay deal with the unions … That complicates matters.'

You say that your hands were tied by circumstances but the governor shows little sympathy.

'We'll do what we have to do,' he says when the meeting ends, in a tone that sounds like a warning. Polly is wondering aloud at his meaning on the drive back to Westminster when June says it's obvious.

'It's just what I said,' she says. 'The Bank's going to increase interest rates. They're already under pressure because inflation is above 2 per cent, and by caving to the unions on pay we've done something that'll make the situation worse.'

'With apologies from this doddery old fool,' Polly says. 'But how does putting up interest rates actually help?'

June points to the dashboard. She says it's like air conditioning. If a car gets too hot – in other words, prices are rising and the economy is booming – you can blast the air conditioning.

'That's like increasing the interest rate,' she says. 'It takes money – heat, so to speak – out of the economy. More people save instead of spend, to take advantage of the higher interest rates. Home owners face higher mortgage payments, so they have less to spend in the shops. Companies with loans also face higher interest payments. Overall, there's less upward pressure on prices. Conversely, if this car started to get too cold – in other words, if prices were rising too slowly and the economy was weak – you could turn down the air conditioning. That's like cutting the interest rate. And the effects go in reverse.'

Polly's expression is pensive and then she grimaces.

'Rough timing,' she says. 'Not the best offer to the public, is it? More expensive mortgages for all! Congratulations, you're now priced out of buying a home! And what about debts on credit cards? People will pay more in interest, won't they?'

She turns to see June nodding.

'Can't the governor just wait until after the election?' Polly asks.

June says that's not how it works. 'The Bank is independent for exactly this reason,' she says. To stop politicians and meddlers like Polly from engineering economic booms just in time for a national vote. Polly dislikes this answer and spends the rest of the car journey in a sullen silence, arms folded.

And it's Polly who comes to you a few days later with a bold idea, as you're preparing your media comment ahead of the Bank's rates decision.

'Chancellor, I think we need to remind people that we're on their side,' she says. 'I fear the governor has lost sight of the difficult economic realities facing the people this government was elected to represent. If rates go up, we have to distance ourselves from the decision. Say that the Bank has got it wrong this time. We can't be seen to be supporting more pain in the pocket for voters in a year like this.'

You notice Polly has made this suggestion to you without June present. You can only imagine she'd strongly counsel the opposite.

The Bank's decision day arrives and yes, as predicted, the governor announces a hike in interest rates, citing 'growing pressures in the labour market' and a 'robust commitment' to returning inflation to the 2 per cent target. Shortly after the announcement, a journalist and a crew with a broadcast camera are waiting for you outside the Treasury.

'Remember,' Polly says. 'This clip will be in all the evening broadcasts. We have to get the message right.'

Suddenly the camera is rolling and the journalist proffers a fluffy microphone.

'So, tell us, chancellor,' they say. 'What's your reaction to the Bank's move today?'

It's time to make your next decision.

DECISION

Criticise the Bank. You think Polly is right. Voters won't be impressed to hear you saying that their outgoings need to increase, especially when times are already hard. You respect the Bank's independence, of course, but there's still a place for healthy criticism of their actions. You also think they've acted prematurely: your public sector pay deal has only just been announced. The Bank should've at least waited to see its impact before hiking rates. If you choose this option, turn to p. 42.

OFFICIAL – SENSITIVE

DECISION

Support the Bank. You think Polly is wrong. You agree with June that the Bank's independence is important, and you don't want to be seen to be saying anything that suggests otherwise. You support the idea of controlling inflation, and if that means hiking interest rates, then so be it. You also think the public understands this, so the political risk of supporting the Bank is limited. If you choose this option, turn to p. 44.

OFFICIAL – SENSITIVE

YOU CRITICISE THE BANK

You say that you respect the Bank's efforts to control inflation, but you question whether now is the right time to be
raising rates. You can see Polly nodding vigorously behind
the journalist. You conclude by saying you'll do everything in
your power to bring down the cost of living, and that you'll
work to ease the pain of higher rates.

'Perfect,' Polly says, as you re-enter the Treasury. 'That'll
tell 'em.'

But what you considered a rather anodyne comment
suddenly snowballs, your message of support for the public
immediately forgotten.

'Did the chancellor just try to put political pressure on
the Bank?' one famous financial commentator asks online.
The shadow chancellor – your main political opponent in the
House of Commons – replies to the question with: 'Unaccept-
able interference here. The chancellor should know better.'

You're watching the reaction online blow up when Polly
pokes her head sheepishly around your office door. She says
the press team is getting inundated by journalists asking
whether the governor still has your full support.

'Of course he does,' you say, alarmed at how this has esca-
lated. Then you see a Sky News breaking alert: 'Chancellor
Attacks BOE Governor over "Painful" Rate Hikes'.

You ask Polly: 'Attacks? Did we really attack him?'

'No,' she says, palm to her forehead. 'But the media loves to sensationalise.'

June joins you with a look of disdain, her arms tightly folded.

'Next time we want to criticise *the central bank of the United Kingdom*, please seek my advice first,' she says. 'And I come bearing more bad news.'

June explains that she's seen the Treasury's latest modelling for how the increase in interest rates will affect your budget surplus.

'There are two problems,' she says. 'First, higher debt interest payments. It's not just more expensive for the man and woman on the street to borrow. It's more expensive for us too.'

You're reminded of that chunky slice of the government spending pie labelled 'debt interest' that you saw on your tour with Sir Alex. If that's got bigger, all else being equal, you can see you now have less to spend on public services.

'And second, the health of the economy itself,' June says. 'Higher interest rates depress the economy, like we talked about in the car. And since the economy will be weaker – lower salaries, lower profits, lower spending – we're going to have lower tax receipts. Less income tax, less tax from companies, less tax from VAT. You get the picture.'

'I feel less bad about shading the governor now,' Polly says.

You give a grim smile, rueing that this is how your first interaction with the Bank of England has played out. And your apparent rift with the governor doesn't go unnoticed by the public: the opposition continue to make much of it in the coming days and polls show a hit to your reputation.

Deduct £4 billion from your budget surplus and one point from your approval rating. Now turn to p. 46.

YOU SUPPORT THE BANK

To Polly's disappointment, you say that you fully support the governor's actions and that the Treasury and Bank are totally united in their desire to bring down inflation. You say you recognise the concerns about the cost of living but remain resolutely committed to economic stability.

You're in your office later that afternoon when June joins you, saying she has an important update. She asks if you know what's wrong with Polly and you explain the cause of her sour face.

'Wow,' June says. 'Thank goodness you didn't listen to her. It's rule number one of being chancellor. Don't criticise the governor. Have your disagreements in private, yes, but never in public. That was a bullet dodged.'

June hands you a briefing note and says she's nevertheless sorry to be the bearer of bad news. She explains that the hike in interest rates will reduce your budget surplus: the government's debt interest payments are due to be higher, and the economy will grow less than expected because of the depressive effect of higher borrowing costs for companies and households.

'Lower growth means lower tax receipts,' she says. 'And that means less money for us. It's obviously a setback.'

You thank her for the update, expressing a note of trepidation that your economic position can take such a turn on factors outside your control.

'Welcome to the vagaries of being chancellor,' she says.

**Deduct £4 billion from your budget surplus.
Now turn to p. 46.**

CHAPTER 6

Mansion House

*It was probably the highlight
of the year, apart from the Budget.*
Philip Hammond on the chancellor's Mansion House speech

You're still digesting the implications of the Bank's interest rate hike as you walk back to No. 11 Downing Street that evening when you get a panicked message from Polly: 'Chancellor, can I come over? Turns out we've got a big problem next week.'

You check your watch: it's 8.30pm. Certainly, you reply, already having surrendered to the total blurring of the work–life balance that comes with running the UK economy from your home that's also an office. You take your ministerial box to the No. 11 study and Polly soon joins you.

'Not to impose an essay crisis on you, chancellor,' Polly says. 'But I was checking in with Sir Alex and some of the officials earlier on Mansion House. And guess what. There's zero material for the speech. *Zero*. It's currently a blank page.'

You feel falling in your stomach. Mansion House – the chancellor's annual address to the City where the government details its plans for the all-important financial services sector

– is your first big speech in the role. You really want to make a good impression and the idea that you're starting from scratch is mildly terrifying.

'Not to worry though,' Polly says. 'I've lit a bonfire under the officials. We'll do a big meeting tomorrow and sort it. June's cracking the whip too.'

Hence you find yourself in the No. 11 dining room the following afternoon, surrounded by your advisors and civil servants, with various ideas on the table. The grandeur of Soane's architecture feels like an appropriate setting for determining the future of one of the jewels of Britain's economy.

'Forgive us that preparations on the speech are not quite as advanced as you might have expected, chancellor,' Sir Alex says. 'However, once again, the lack of direction from your predecessor meant we lacked sufficient ministerial guidance. I'm sure this will be swiftly corrected.'

It emerges from the discussion that you have two options. The first is to take a clear pro-City stance, signalling your support for various reforms that would boost the UK finance sector. Ideas include creating a special visa to encourage the richest people to come to Britain, offering banks more leeway to make riskier investments and giving the government powers to overrule the financial regulator if they deem a decision will hold back the economy. June is the strongest advocate for this approach.

'Finance is one of the things we do best,' she says, reeling off the well-known list of advantages that have cemented Britain as a world leader in the field: the favourable time zone bridging West and East, English as a global language, the strength and independence of Britain's judicial system, the wealth of well-educated professionals, London's thriving cultural scene, and so on. 'Finance makes up more than 10 per cent of the entire UK economy and employs 2.5 million people,' she points out. 'We should double down on all this,' she says. 'Supercharge our comparative advantage.'

Your second option – most vocally backed by Polly – is to take a more cautious view on the City, emphasising the highest standards of regulation, close alignment with the European Union and scoring populist hits like reintroducing a cap on bankers' bonuses.

'We need to show the little man we're on their side,' she says. 'Going after the fat cats. And not letting the City take the big risks that left us bailing them out back in '08.'

'Times have changed,' June counters. 'Financial systems are far more resilient nowadays. If anything, the world went too far the other way after the global financial crisis. We can begin to correct that.'

You look to Sir Alex and notice a frown of remembrance. You can only imagine the stresses he went through at that time in the Treasury, when the world economy teetered on the brink of collapse as banks buckled under the weight of toxic assets and debts, needing billions of pounds in emergency government rescue packages to avert social breakdown.

'Whatever you decide, chancellor, our brilliant speech-writers will have a draft for you in no time,' Sir Alex says. 'And with any luck, you won't make as big a stir as Lloyd George.'

Sir Alex grins at your blank expression.

'The most famous Mansion House speech of all, in 1911, chancellor,' he says. 'Germany had just deployed a gunboat off the coast of Morocco to protect its colonial interests in the build-up to the First World War, seen as a provocation by Britain and France. Lloyd George said it was a threat to national honour and the security of international trade. The German ambassador called his remarks a thunderbolt.'

Polly jokes that we could only dream of making so historic an intervention.

'There's a challenge for the press office,' she says, slapping one of the officials on the back.

You're mulling over the merits of each approach in your study alone later that evening, working through your red box, when you come to the memo on the Mansion House speech. It's time to make your decision.

DECISION

Take the pro-City stance. You agree with June. You want to do everything you can to boost the performance of the City. It's one of the UK's strongest assets and a major source of tax revenues. Yes, it may mean accepting more risk in the financial system, but it'll be worth it for the chance of improved returns. You want to encourage even more investment into Britain, and this will send a positive signal to the world. If you choose this option, turn to p. 52.

OFFICIAL – SENSITIVE

DECISION

Take the cautious City stance. You agree with Polly. Your first concern is the views of voters, and you imagine it will go down well if you take a swing at overpaid bankers. You also think it's reasonable to keep the City on a tight leash. We've seen who ultimately pays when things go wrong in the world of finance – the taxpayer – and you want to minimise those risks. If you choose this option, turn to p. 55.

YOU TAKE THE PRO-CITY STANCE

You're standing in your finest evening wear in the Egyptian Hall of Mansion House – a grand banquet of the City's great and the good before you, a marble statue of Comus, Greek deity of festivity and revelry, looking on – when there's a collective hush. The Lord Mayor of London, holder of one of the world's oldest civic offices, has just introduced you, the Bank of England governor sitting alongside. You rise to your feet and adjust your notes, taking in the splendour of the occasion: the beautiful nineteenth-century stained-glass windows high above, the towering Roman columns topped with gold, the ornate barrel-domed ceiling. If ever there's a scene that captures the opulence, wealth and history of the City, you think, then this is it.

What you remember best when you're back at No. 11 Downing Street that evening, relieved that it's all over, is the sound. The sound of the tentative silence of your opening that became a low-level approving murmur. The sound of the first pop of a champagne bottle, bringing a gale of laughter. The sound of the celebratory chinking of glasses as you announced yet another pro-City initiative, swelling to a general bonhomie and delight as the assorted captains of British finance realised who you were. An ally and a champion of their world.

'It couldn't really have gone any better,' you tell Polly in your study the next morning. But she's pulling a funny face.

'I'm guessing you haven't seen the papers,' she says, laying out the editorial pages of *The Times*, *Guardian* and *Daily Mail*. You start with the *Guardian*.

Chancellor's Love-In with the Bankers Is a Slap in the Face for Ordinary Brits

With people up and down the UK struggling to pay their bills, few sights are more galling than that of our new chancellor quaffing champagne with the masters of the universe last night. In their alternative reality of caviar and bumper bonuses, the chancellor missed the opportunity to remind those gathered of their duties to society in these difficult times. Instead of prudent calls for caution and temperance, we saw the encouragement of all the worst excesses that landed this country in the sort of trouble our politicians swore we'd never see again.

Then you turn to *The Times*.

CHANCELLOR MISSES THE MOOD WITH CHUMMY MANSION HOUSE ADDRESS

This paper is all in favour of the City and its enormous contribution to our economy. But there is a time and a place for the kind of bullish optimism displayed by our chancellor last night, and a braying banquet of Britain's elite whilst the rest of the country struggles is neither. Politics is about optics as much as anything else, and it seems ill-judged to have been so cosy and at ease with the decadence on display at Mansion House.

Polly puts her hand over the *Daily Mail*.

'Actually best you don't read that one,' she says. 'You get the gist.'

Polly is trying to reassure you that no-one really reads newspapers anymore anyway when you're joined by June, who gives you a thumbs-up.

'Great speech, chancellor,' she says. 'So great, in fact, that I come with good news.'

June explains that she's been discussing your Mansion House reforms with the Treasury's in-house economists, and they reckon your plans will lift the economy and in turn increase your budget surplus. She says they need to wait for official confirmation from the relevant authorities, but we can reasonably assume at least a £1 billion boost to our financial position.

'Tell the *Daily Mail* to print that,' she says.

Deduct 1 point from your approval rating and increase your budget surplus by £1 billion. Now turn to p. 57.

YOU TAKE THE CAUTIOUS CITY STANCE

It's a relief that the Egyptian Hall of Mansion House is such a sight to behold – the glorious nineteenth-century stained-glass windows, the towering Roman columns, an intricate barrel-domed ceiling – because you'd rather look anywhere in this room than at the glum, verging-on-hostile sea of faces at the glamorous banquet in front of you, Britain's captains of industry listening in a stony silence. Your insistence on the highest standards of financial regulation elicits the first cough. Your reminder of the dangers of excessive risk-taking and the human costs of the global financial crisis is met with awkward glances away and much lap-gazing. Your trepidation grows as you build to the big final announcement of your speech – the cap on bankers' bonuses – and you were right to be afraid: you're met with instant mutterings of 'shame' and even provoke a heckle.

'What do you politicians know about making money?' one man in a fine tuxedo stands to say, a drained glass of champagne in his wavering hand. 'About building a business? About taking risks? Parasites, every one of you.'

You're pinching the bridge of your nose as your ministerial car whisks you back to Downing Street afterwards when Polly leans over to show you her phone.

'I know that was pretty awkward,' she says. 'But look how it's being reported. The wasted heckler was a godsend.'

'Parasites?' one well-known commentator has tweeted. 'Talk about a monumental lack of self-awareness. Credit to the chancellor for taking a tough stance tonight.'

Others are calling your speech 'brave' and 'necessary'. Another famous political pundit puts it thus: 'The chancellor went into the lion's den tonight and gave them a bloody nose. That was refreshing.'

You're basking in the glow of the positive press coverage the next morning when June joins you in your study. She'd also been necking the champagne last night, but shows no sign of a hangover.

'I see last night went down well,' she says. 'However, something to flag. The Treasury economists are saying our Mansion House package will likely hit our surplus. You know how it is: the wealthy are fleet of foot and the likes of Dubai, Hong Kong and New York become much more attractive when we're capping bonuses. And if many bankers leave, it'll reduce our tax take. So they're modelling a £1 billion reduction in our position. I agree with them.'

She offers a parting thought before she turns to leave.

'Chancellor, I'm sure you're aware of this,' she says. 'But let's be careful about biting the hand that feeds.'

Add one point to your approval rating and deduct £1 billion from your surplus. Now turn to p. 57.

CHAPTER 7

Meeting the Boss

The chancellor's power derives from their
relationship with the prime minister.
Kwasi Kwarteng, Chancellor of the Exchequer,
September–October 2022

Quite remarkably, with Christmas approaching and as you enter your sixth week as chancellor, the moment finally arrives: your first private meeting with the prime minister in 10 Downing Street since your appointment.

Normally you'd aim to meet at least weekly, but in between the PM's manic schedule and extensive international travel – her Middle East visit, an unexpected trip to the United Nations in New York and then an international summit in Delhi – plus your own unavailability as you've got to grips with the Treasury, it's only now that your packed diaries have aligned.

'Chancellor,' she says, welcoming you with a warm embrace, inviting you to sit next to her in the Cabinet room, perhaps the most significant room in all of British history. 'It's been too long. And we have so much to discuss.'

It still feels surreal to you that the woman beside you – her name is Emily Edwards – also happens to be the Prime

Minister of the United Kingdom. You've known and seen Emily in guises and locations far less grandiose than this. This is the Emily who staggered home with you 12 years earlier, arm draped around your shoulder after a boozy networking event for prospective parliamentary candidates and an impromptu round of clubbing where she'd tactically vomited in a hedge and you'd instantly become friends. It's the lady with whom you knocked on doors in the freezing wind and rain as you both sought election, maintaining morale by belting eighties classics and eating her questionable home-baked chocolate muffins. This is the Emily with whom you used to sit in the tea room of the House of Commons, talking inanities and exchanging notes on which of your fellow new MPs you fancied.

But in another sense, you always felt an aura about Emily that made her political ascent seem inevitable. The way heads would turn to her when she entered a room, even if she was the most junior person present. The way she'd glide around social occasions, making everyone feel special with a remembered personal detail or ready amusing anecdote. The range in her voice: weighty and with gravitas when needed, but then bubbly and charismatic the next. Her turn of phrase, too, an ability to distil political ideas into simple slogans that would mimic the thoughts of voters. When she put her name forward for the party leadership, you had no hesitation in giving her your support. Indeed, you canvassed hard for her, sensing you were backing a winner and seeing the prospect of future personal reward.

'As you know,' Emily says, tapping the table, a portrait of Britain's first prime minister, Robert Walpole, watching over her. 'Big year coming up. Big, big year. The year of our next stunning electoral success.'

A smile passes between you. The date of the next general election is a secret known only to you and Emily. She's planning to call it in the autumn, just after your Budget. She says she doesn't believe the polls are really as close as they are – 'we're on the side of common-sense Britain', that's her catchphrase – and her confidence is on full display.

'I'm thinking the triple whammy,' she says. 'Blockbuster speech in the New Year with a big crowd-pleasing policy. Another gift to the public at your Spring Statement. And then the home run at the Budget.'

Emily's optimism and energy are one of her great strengths, the infectious sparkle in her eyes when animated by an idea or a plan. That sparkle is there now when she comes to her flagship idea for her New Year speech.

'Immigration,' she says. 'I think we need a real offer on immigration. Something to silence our political opponents. Show the public that we're taking action once and for all.'

Emily slides you a dossier, prompting subtle looks of consternation among your Treasury officials sat around the room. Bilateral meetings between the prime minister and chancellor are prepared meticulously in advance by your respective teams and evidently this document is unexpected.

'I've got all the details here,' she says. 'The plan is a very strict cap on visas. No more than a few thousand each year. The situation of hundreds of thousands of people coming just can't carry on. The pressure on our schools, hospitals, roads, infrastructure ... I think it'll be a real vote-winner. Of course, I'm expecting this will have your full backing. Won't it?'

You're just about to answer when Sir Alex speaks, an intervention that says much about his seniority and legendary authority in the civil service. You can count on one hand the number of people in the British state who would dare to have spoken up at that moment.

'Forgive me for the interruption, prime minister,' he says. 'I've been alerted to an urgent matter that requires the chancellor's immediate attention. If I may.'

Sir Alex ushers you into the Cabinet anteroom, the place where ministers assemble as they wait to join the weekly meeting to run the country. It's decorated by a painting of the original Whitehall Palace that was destroyed by fire at the end of the seventeenth century, a sobering reminder of the fragility of power.

'Chancellor, I fear we have been ambushed,' Sir Alex whispers. 'I'd strongly advise against giving any kind of immediate assent to the prime minister's proposal. Not first without careful consideration of its impact. I am sure the Treasury will be able to give you chapter and verse on the merits and demerits of immigration. This is a policy area that calls for sober reflection.'

You apologise to Emily for the interlude when you return and say you'll have to study the plan in detail. Your answer is non-committal when she asks if the idea nevertheless has your initial support. And that's when you see the flash behind the eyes. Because for all of Emily's charm and charisma, her swagger and common touch, the friendship you've shared over more than a decade, you're well aware that she also has a ruthless streak, a ferocious ambition and drive that paved her path to becoming the most powerful person in the country. You've heard Emily be rude to her staff. You've seen her shout at officials who've made mistakes. You've known her to brief viciously against her opponents, to the point of inventing lies. And that was the Emily you saw in that fleeting moment, the single-minded political operator behind the sweet public visage who will do whatever it takes to attain and retain this office. It's why there's a part of you that has never fully trusted her.

'Naturally,' Emily says, face and tone fully recomposed, speaking as if your answer was eminently reasonable. 'Take your time. I only want to do this if it has your full buy-in.' Then she laughs. 'But maybe don't take too long. I'm planning to put the idea to Cabinet tomorrow. I'm sure you'll be with me.'

Sir Alex is wiping a chequered handkerchief across his forehead as you make the short walk back to the Treasury afterwards, his expression pained.

'That was definitely an ambush,' he says. 'Typical No. 10. Trying to bounce us into policies with significant cost implications without appropriate scrutiny. She knew what she was doing. Now, you might think the prime minister's idea is a good one. But please, only make that judgement once I've shown you the numbers.'

And with that, Sir Alex is belying his age and jogging up the steps to the Treasury. You quicken your step to follow.

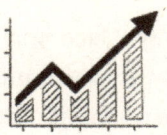

CHAPTER 8

Immigration Nation

You have to respect the office of the
prime minister. They're your boss.
Jeremy Hunt

An emergency gathering of officials and number-crunchers is hastily convened in your office in the Treasury. Sir Alex is leading proceedings with another swiftly secured white-board, civil servants crammed onto the red sofas. He begins with a concession.

'The prime minister is right about one thing,' he says. 'Many, many people have come to Britain in recent years. Voila.'

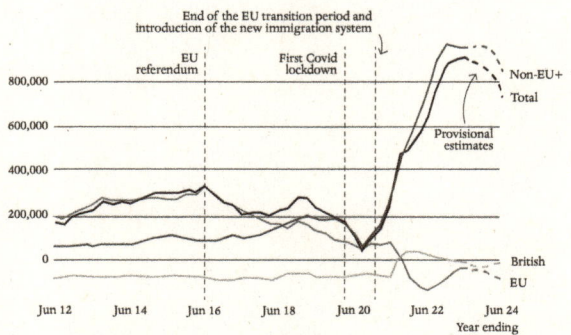

Long-term international migration, provisional

'This is net migration. It's the number of people who came to the UK in a given one-year period minus the number who left. As you can see, huge numbers. In the 200,000s annually between 2012 and 2020. And then surging even further after we completed our split from the European Union. Look at that. In the year to June 2023: 906,000. The population of the UK growing by more than 1 per cent in a year due to immigration.'

Polly asks about Brexit. Wasn't that meant to cut these numbers? Take back control?

'We did take back control of our borders,' Sir Alex says. 'We just made crossing them very easy through a generous visa scheme.'

You can see Polly's eyes lighting up with enthusiasm for the prime minister's proposal, her mental gears whirring about how she'd spin it: British jobs for British workers, shorter queues in A&E, less traffic on the M25, more school places for your children ... But then Sir Alex is giving his warning.

'The danger here is the hit to the public finances,' he says. 'Migrants make a significant contribution to society and the economy. Our National Health Service and care homes would be in a far worse state than they already are if it wasn't for the work of migrants. The skill shortages that are stymying companies up and down the country would be even more acute. Migrants are an essential lifeblood of the economy, especially in an aging, increasingly sick population where more and more people are reliant on welfare. Someone needs to go out there and get the work done which we can then tax and spend on public services. Migrants are essential.'

June joins the discussion, pointing out that your current budget surplus assumes a continuation of high levels of net migration. 'Going ahead with the prime minister's plan would inevitably hit the surplus,' she says, predicting that the relevant statistical authorities would downgrade their expectations for the British economy due to a reduction in the pool of productive workers. She says officials are forecasting a £3 billion hit from the PM's proposal.

'I doubt we want that in an election year,' she says.

You walk into the Cabinet room the next day – a place where decisions affecting millions of people in the UK and beyond have been made since the 1700s – still undecided on what to do. You take your seat at the boat-shaped table opposite the prime minister, introduced by Harold Macmillan in the early 1960s and designed as such so that she can see all her senior ministers without leaning forward. The room feels far more claustrophobic now as you sit shoulder to shoulder with your fellow members of the government. The prime minister begins by wishing everyone a very happy Christmas and offers a bullish round-up of everything they've achieved over the last 12 months.

'But we cannot slacken the pace,' she says. 'Hence we're all systems go into next year. An election year, no less.'

There is much banging on the table and acclamations of 'hear hear' at mention of the vote. In your nervousness, you do not partake.

'Which brings me to the big New Year's speech,' the prime minister continues. 'As some of you may know, I'm considering a significant policy announcement on immigration. Colleagues will obviously have strong views on this issue, but I'm sure we can arrive at a united position. Remember. Divided parties lose elections.'

The prime minister takes a moment to look everyone around the table in the eye, her gaze settling on you. Her look is expectant and artful.

'Chancellor,' she says. 'What do you think of the plan?'

It's time to make your next decision.

DECISION

Support the prime minister's proposal. You're alive to the potential negative economic impact, but you agree that this would be a policy to seize the nation's attention and show you're taking action on an issue of public concern. You're also aware of how keen the prime minister is on the plan, and want to maintain good relations with her. *Deduct £3 billion from your surplus.* If you choose this option, turn to p. 66.

Oppose the prime minister's proposal. You're sympathetic to the idea that immigration is too high, but you think the prime minister's solution is too drastic and will do economic harm that the country can ill-afford. You're trying to build up a strong position with an eye on your Budget, and this initiative would undermine that. You expect the prime minister won't be pleased, but it's your job to stand up for what's best for the public finances. *No cost.* If you choose this option, turn to p. 69.

OFFICIAL – SENSITIVE

YOU SUPPORT THE
PRIME MINISTER'S PROPOSAL

You say you think it's a brilliant idea, just the kind of policy that will steal the front pages and give lift-off to the election campaign. 'Start as we mean to go on,' you say.

The prime minister clenches her fist with delight.

'Superb,' she says. 'Anyone else?'

Your backing triggers near universal support from the rest of the table. These politicians aren't fools: once the prime minister and chancellor have decided on a course of action, only a brave government minister would suggest anything else.

The New Year rolls round and you find yourself on a shared stage with the prime minister in the media suite of 9 Downing Street, announcing the plan to a live press conference with the cameras rolling and the nation's top journalists in attendance.

'But chancellor, aren't you concerned about what this will do to the British economy?' asks the political editor of the *Financial Times*.

You don't need to check your notes before answering, this being the answer you'd rehearsed most. You say that this plan is actually a vote of confidence in Britain. Confidence in the talent and industry of the British people to step up and fill any job vacancies. Confidence in the capacity of British businesses and the British education system to provide the training and skills necessary to plug any shortages. 'It's time we stood on our own two feet,' you say. 'We must resist the temptation of the easy option of immigration.' The prime minister turns to you and says she couldn't have put it better herself.

The prime minister's mood improves further in the days following when she sees the reaction to the plan: the papers lap it up and you get a healthy bump in the polls.

'Finally, Control' declares the *Sun*.

'An End to Open-Door Britain' is the verdict of the *Daily Mail*.

'The White Cliffs of No-Ver' says the *Daily Express*, complete with a mock-up of you and the prime minister flicking the V sign towards the English Channel. Polly likes that one so much that she cuts out a copy and sticks it up in your study.

You're basking in the warm glow of public approval that weekend – the positive coverage continues into the Sunday papers – when June asks to see you in No. 11. She seems worried.

'Chancellor, we both know how tight the public finances are,' she says, entering your study with eyes downcast. 'And I've got no doubt we'll face big pressure from No. 10 to deliver tax cuts before the election. All I'm saying is, we need to be careful. We'll definitely get turfed out if we lose our grip on the economy.'

You thank June for her counsel and reassure her you've got everything under control. As she's leaving, your phone lights up with another message from the prime minister.

She's forwarded you yet another poll showing you pulling ahead of the opposition. She's written: 'Five more years! Five more years!'

Add two points to your approval rating.
Now turn to p. 71.

YOU OPPOSE THE
PRIME MINISTER'S PROPOSAL

You say that you share the prime minister's concerns about immigration, but fear that her plan is an overcorrection which will hurt the economy. To her dismay, your comments have a domino-like effect around the table, with other ministers also piping up with misgivings. 'What about the effect on the number of doctors in the NHS?' asks the health secretary. 'Companies are already struggling with labour shortages,' notes the business secretary. 'And it'll be years before we're ready to plug the skills gaps,' says the education secretary. The prime minister thanks everyone for their feedback.

'We'll keep thinking on this one,' she says, eyeing you coldly. 'But I'd remind colleagues that we need to show the ambition that the public expects from us. We serve only at their pleasure.'

June is congratulating you on having taken a stand the next morning when Polly enters your study in No. 11 and says she's had a worrying call from a journalist.

'It's leaked,' she says. 'The Cabinet split. *The Times* has it. They're saying you orchestrated a revolt against the PM's plan.'

Orchestrated a revolt! You say that's putting it rather too strongly. You'd simply pointed out your reasonable concerns which others shared.

'That's what I'll tell them,' she says. 'But I bet the nuance gets lost.'

Polly's fears are well founded. The write-up on the front page of the next day's *Times* tells a story of a bean-counting Treasury and inflexible chancellor who have stood in the way of a brilliant immigration plan devised by the prime minister, the piece littered with 'allies' of the PM criticising your judgement and labelling you an obstructionist and a blocker.

'I simply have no idea where any of this has come from,' the prime minister says to you in a message, at which Polly rolls her eyes. 'I will reiterate to colleagues the utmost importance of the secrecy of Cabinet and our duty of collective responsibility.'

Yet the *Times* piece triggers a wave of negative coverage in the press, the narrative taking hold that you're the reason the immigration plan floundered. Political cartoonists mock you up unflatteringly holding open a door, the caption reading: 'Roll up! Roll up! Britain open to all.'

'It's such dirty tricks from No. 10,' Polly says, as the media fallout extends into a second week. 'We really have to watch our backs, chancellor.'

Deduct two points from your approval rating.
Now turn to p. 71.

CHAPTER 9

It's the Economy, Stupid

*The best thing for fiscal sustainability
is a healthy, growing economy.*
Rachel Reeves

There's very little respite in the frantic schedule of the chancellor, and the next Monday morning finds you in the first-class carriage of a train speeding to Darlington, heading to the Treasury's economic campus in the north. You're working through your red box – signing off spending decisions, giving instructions to your officials, rolling countryside whizzing by – when your interest is piqued by the lively conversation between Polly and June on the table beside you. They're meant to be preparing your media statement for the next day's GDP (gross domestic product) figures – a measure of the size of the economy calculated by adding up the value of all the goods and services being produced in a society.

'I just don't get why there's always this obsession with growing it,' Polly says. She's giving you the side eye, enjoying the chance to wind up June. 'Can't we just be happy with the GDP we've got?'

'No,' June snaps. 'Not with a growing population like ours. It's like a pie. Imagine you and your friend are sharing a pie. You get half each. Now imagine there are four of you. Would you personally get the same amount of pie? No. You'd get less. And it's the same with the economy and our collective prosperity. If the economy stands still while the population is growing, it means we'd all get less individually. What we're talking about here is GDP per capita. Per person. And obviously we want that to grow. We want people to feel better off. That's how we win elections, right?'

'Now I'm listening,' Polly says. She gets even more excited when June explains how improving GDP numbers boost your budget surplus. 'When the economy is doing better – people earning higher salaries, businesses making bigger profits – then the government takes in more revenue in tax,' June says. 'And that means more money to spend on public services and for giveaways to voters.'

'So yes,' June says. 'You certainly should care about GDP.'

You're particularly interested in the state of your current budget surplus because of your next upcoming set-piece: the Spring Statement, a moment where you update the nation on the health of the public finances and have the opportunity to announce new economic policies. Often called a mini-Budget, it'll be your first big speech in the House of Commons with all eyes in Westminster watching. The prime minister's expectation when you spoke in the Cabinet room still rings in your ears: *'Another gift to the public at your Spring Statement ...'*

'Let's hope tomorrow's numbers are good,' June says, reading your concern. 'I expect we'll need all the firepower we can get.'

To your pleasant surprise, the numbers are indeed good. The Office for National Statistics (ONS) announces that the

British economy grew faster than expected in the previous quarter, a nice gift from your predecessor. June notes that the impact of the Bank of England's interest rate hike may take a little time to feed into the economy, but for now this is certainly good news.

'Maybe we'll be able to afford a tax cut after all,' June says.

Add £5 billion to your budget surplus.
Now turn to p. 74.

CHAPTER 10

Enter the OBR

The OBR is a very, very powerful force.
Kwasi Kwarteng

A special kind of energy infuses the Treasury in the run-up to an event like the Spring Statement – a fiscal event, as it's called – a tangible buzz as the well-oiled machine of the civil service stirs into action: policy teams proposing ideas for the speech, economists costing those ideas, the communications team drawing up media strategies, plans being mooted then scrapped, regular dialogues with No. 10, all in a constant iterative process managed by you and your team as you edge towards the big day.

Crucial to the whole process, however, is the role of the Office for Budget Responsibility (OBR), an independent watchdog established by former chancellor George Osborne in 2010. They produce the official economic forecasts which confirm how much money you have to play with, and that's what you're anxiously awaiting one afternoon as you sit in your study in No. 11 Downing Street with Polly and June.

'I say who cares what the OBR thinks,' Polly says, whispering in June's ear, as June keeps refreshing her emails and mutters about the importance of sticking to the fiscal rules. 'Who needs fiscal rules anyway?'

'Don't try me,' June says. 'Just read the memo.'

June has helpfully prepared a cheat sheet on the fiscal rules, which you run through now. The rules are targets you impose upon yourself to signal your economic credibility. They're like guardrails, a promise to investors and the markets that you won't let spending or government debt get out of control. Different governments have adopted different fiscal rules at different times, but they all serve the same purpose. June explains that the budget surplus figure you've been tracking is your buffer against your fiscal rules, otherwise known as your headroom. June says that we risk the wrath of financial markets if we blow out our headroom.

'It's here!' June says, beckoning you both to crowd around her laptop. 'OBR forecasts. Let's take a look.'

It's time to take stock of your economic position.

If your budget surplus is £9 billion or higher, turn to p. 76. If your budget surplus is £8 billion or lower, turn to p. 77.

YOUR BUDGET SURPLUS IS
£9 BILLION OR HIGHER

'Not bad,' June says. 'Not bad at all.'

You read through the OBR's summary with cautious optimism. Their forecasts tally with the numbers you've been working on from the in-house Treasury economists, and they show that you're currently meeting your fiscal rules with respectable room to spare. You'd heard horror stories of past chancellors being thrown into disarray by a sudden swing in the numbers from the OBR, but that's not happened here.

'So it's full steam ahead to the Spring Statement,' Polly says. 'Tax cuts galore.'

'Steady on,' June says. She points to the line in the OBR analysis about how your headroom is still low by historical standards. Chancellors averaged £28 billion of headroom between 2010 and 2024, she notes. 'We're still pretty vulnerable to shocks and need to be careful. But yes. It could definitely be worse.'

You're combing through the fine print of the OBR numbers when you then receive a message from the prime minister.

'Quick catch-up in No. 10?'

Now turn to p. 78.

YOUR BUDGET SURPLUS IS
£8 BILLION OR LOWER

'Not ideal,' June says. 'Definitely not ideal.'

There's some good news in the OBR's summary – you're still on course to meet your fiscal rules, and their assessment of your surplus is the same as the one you've been working on from your in-house Treasury economists – but their tone is downbeat and cautious. The watchdog is warning that you're running your headroom dangerously low, and that it could easily be wiped out by a downturn in the economy or some other shock. They say that chancellors had an average headroom of £28 billion between 2010 and 2024, and you're clearly far from those levels of comfort. They also point out that this forecast applies even before you've presented them with any policies you're considering for your Spring Statement.

'So no giveaways then?' Polly asks.

'Well, it just means we have to be really careful,' June says. 'But yes. We're pretty restricted.'

You're studying the OBR's analysis with a frown when you get a message from the prime minister.

'Quick catch-up in No. 10?'

Now turn to p. 78.

CHAPTER 11

The Tax Cut

*The chancellor, in addition to saying no
to colleagues, occasionally has to
say no to the prime minister.*
Norman Lamont

You make the short interior walk from No. 11 to No. 10 and find the prime minister in her study, a portrait of Margaret Thatcher looking on. She asks her officials to leave so that you can speak in private.

'So then,' she says, eyes gleaming with a plan. 'Spring Statement. We need something good. What do you think?'

You're about to start with the OBR's numbers but she's already speaking over you.

'I was thinking VAT,' she says. 'Nice big tax cut. Everyone benefits. Easy to understand. Helps with the cost of living. The papers would love it.'

VAT – value added tax, a 20 per cent levy on most goods and services – is one of the government's biggest earners. You remember Sir Alex's pie chart: it brings in about 17 per cent of all government tax revenue. It's one of the Treasury's favourite taxes because it's simple to administer and very hard to avoid paying at the till. The prime minister says she wants to cut VAT by 1 percentage point.

'Of course, we'd like to go further,' she says. 'But I know the finances are pretty tight. I think this strikes a good balance. It's the perfect policy in an election year. Don't you agree?'

You're discussing the idea with Polly in your study later that afternoon – you'd successfully been vague with the prime minister about whether you supported her plan, saying you wanted to double-check the numbers first – when you're joined by Sir Alex. He comes armed with a dossier of economic analysis.

'The top-line figure is £9 billion, chancellor,' he says. 'That's what our VAT specialist estimates it would cost.'

Polly's enthusiasm for the idea matches the prime minister's. She says it's a great opportunity to show you're on the side of ordinary Britons and are doing everything you can to make life easier. She also repeats her scepticism of the OBR, saying we should have confidence in our plans and prioritise the politics.

You're weighing up the affordability of the tax cut when Polly's phone vibrates with a notification. She gasps.

'Looks like the decision's already been made for us,' she says, showing you her screen. It's a breaking news story in the *Financial Times*.

Exclusive: Chancellor Prepares VAT Cut in Spring Pre-Election Giveaway

The Treasury is drawing up dramatic plans to cut VAT in the upcoming Spring Statement, a bold give- away to voters ahead of the general election expected later this year.

cont. on p.80

> The chancellor is preparing to announce a 1 percentage point cut to VAT as part of the spring economic update, according to a senior government figure. 'The government wants to deliver the tax cut to help people with the cost of living,' the person said.

'How have they got this already?' Polly asks. 'And who's this senior government figure?'

You're wondering just the same. You explain that it was only yourself and the prime minister present when she raised the idea. And you've only told Polly and Sir Alex since.

'I will of course do a leak inquiry,' Sir Alex says. 'But I doubt this has come from the Treasury. If I had to hazard a guess, then this "senior government figure" is perhaps the most senior government figure of them all.'

You share a look with Polly, weighing Sir Alex's meaning. Polly says that this really changes your calculation. 'Expectations have now been raised enormously with the public,' she says. 'If we don't go through with this tax cut, it'll be terribly embarrassing.'

It's time to make your next decision.

DECISION

Go ahead with the VAT cut. You agree with the prime minister that this is a great pre-election giveaway. It's a policy that's easily understood, will grab the headlines and ease the cost-of-living burden. And the fact that it's been leaked to the press gives you all the more reason to follow through. It's an expensive tax cut, but it'll be worth it for the kudos you'll gain with voters. *Deduct £9 billion from your surplus.* Now turn to p. 82.

Don't cut VAT. You'd like to have a big offer for voters, but you decide that the money simply isn't there. It's your job to keep a tight grip on the public finances and say no when necessary, no matter what's being published in the media. And in any case, you've still got the Budget later this year to do pre-election giveaways. *No cost.* Now turn to p. 84.

OFFICIAL – SENSITIVE

YOU GO AHEAD WITH THE VAT CUT

It's 11.25am on a Tuesday and you're sitting nervously in your parliamentary office in the House of Commons, just yards away from the chamber with its famous green benches, making the final tweaks and revisions to your Spring Statement speech. You can hear a murmur growing as MPs take their seats, anticipation rising. The prime minister pops her head around the door, wishing you luck with a beaming smile.

'The speech is perfect,' she says. 'Just perfect.'

You get a huge cheer when you enter the Commons, a sea of your MPs waving their order papers, all under strict instructions from party high command to be there and in full voice. And then the Speaker – the presiding officer of the chamber – is calling 'Chancellor of the Exchequer!' and you're on your feet, the prime minister propelling you with hearty backslaps and shouts of 'hear hear'.

The lasting visual image you have of the speech afterwards is the glimmer of hope you saw in the eyes of the opposition MPs as you started to wind up, 45 minutes of speech and no tax cut in sight. Then your dramatic pause. Then the grimace of your political opponents and the roar of your own benches at your 'and just one more thing ...'. Everyone in the chamber knows how well this VAT cut will go down on the doorstep ahead of the election. There are few better things a government can do than making everything less expensive. The backslaps from the prime minister are even more emphatic when you finish, the Commons ringing with cheers.

Add three points to your approval rating.

It's now time to do an economic score check.
If your surplus is in the negative, turn to p. 86.
If your surplus is positive, turn to p. 94.

YOU DECIDE NOT TO CUT VAT

The Speaker's voice booms: 'Chancellor of the Exchequer!'

You take to your feet in the House of Commons for your Spring Statement amid a chorus of cheers from your own MPs, but secretly you're dreading the next 45 minutes. Your attempts to downplay the prospect of tax cuts in advance have been written off by the media as typical expectations management by the Treasury, so you really are about to drop an unpleasant surprise. The prime minister hasn't said a word to you all day, sitting in a po-faced silence at your side. You sense from the whispers opposite that your political opponents know something is up. Their mood improves steadily throughout the speech as no tax cuts come, peaking to a crescendo of mocking laughter and finger-pointing when you sit down. They can't believe their luck. To make matters worse, the prime minister immediately walks out of the chamber when you finish, a moment of public division that will feature in all of the evening news bulletins.

The next day's papers make grim reading. 'Was That It, Chancellor?' asks the *Sun*. The *Express* also poses a question: 'VAT Is Going On?' 'PM and Chancellor at War over Tax Cuts,' declares the *Daily Mail*. A silver lining is that you get a slightly more favourable write-up in the financial and business press – commentators say you wisely resisted the allure of expensive populist giveaways to focus on fiscal probity

– but that doesn't prevent a sudden and sizable hit to your approval ratings.

Deduct three points from your approval rating.

It's now time to check your political score.
If your approval rating is 0 or in the negative,
turn to p. 97. If it's more than 0, turn to p. 95.

YOUR SURPLUS HAS TURNED
NEGATIVE AFTER CUTTING VAT

The next day's papers are a sight to behold. It's a clean sweep on your VAT cut and the coverage is overwhelmingly positive. The tabloids are buoyant, declaring you the hero of the hour and a political mastermind who's given your party a pre-election boost.

'Have a Load of VAT!' screams the *Sun*. 'VAT a Gift, Chancellor!' says the *Daily Star*.

But danger lurks on the inside pages of the *Financial Times*, which reports the tremor in markets that happened in the hours after your speech. Several banks published research notes on the sudden lack of credibility in Britain's economic plans, calling the VAT cut 'unfunded' and 'an ill-advised populist giveaway'. This coincided with a pronounced increase in investors ditching UK government debt, a protest vote against your decision.

'It may have been lost in the spectacle and euphoria of the VAT tax cut, but the OBR's assessment is that the chancellor is now on course to breach the fiscal rules,' an analyst for JP Morgan says in the FT article. *'This is very risky behaviour indeed. Don't be surprised if there's a further reaction on the bond markets.'*

Sir Alex enters your office in the Treasury the next morning with a grave look.

'Chancellor, do you remember how I said one never wants to find themselves on an emergency conference call with the Debt and Reserves Management team? Well ... your presence is requested on an emergency conference call with the Debt and Reserves Management team.'

A group of officials updates you on the latest market movements and it's not looking good. There's been a further wave of selling of UK government debt, with market participants taking a collective view that Britain is now a more dangerous bet than before your Spring Statement. Whereas you once had a reputation for fiscal rectitude and competence, investors now see you as a reckless and untrustworthy custodian of the public finances. And with your debt now seen as a riskier prospect, investors are demanding higher and higher interest rates to hold it. This is translating into higher and higher borrowing costs – so your debt interest bill is rising, further worsening your economic position.

'I don't say this lightly, chancellor,' Sir Alex says. 'But we may want to ... swiftly reconsider the Spring Statement package. With an emphasis on swift. This might require what they call a U-turn.'

You ring the prime minister but she's dismissive, still high on the public adulation for the VAT cut. 'Markets go up and markets go down,' she says. 'It'll blow over. These things always do. And we can't be flip-flopping at the first sign of trouble. The public expects us to have a backbone.'

Sir Alex's face is as if he's been sucking a lemon when he hears the PM's response.

'As ever, chancellor,' he says. 'The decision is ultimately yours.'

It's time to make your next choice.

DECISION

Reverse the VAT cut. You're worried about what's playing out on financial markets and fear where it may lead. A U-turn will be a political humiliation, undoubtedly, but doing nothing feels like too great a risk. Reversing the tax cut should restabilise the finances and win back your credibility with investors. *Add £9 billion to your surplus.* Now turn to p. 90.

OFFICIAL – SENSITIVE

DECISION

Keep the VAT cut. You agree with the prime minister that you should stay the course. This is a very popular measure and you're not scared of a little market turbulence. It's not for City speculators and wealthy fund managers to determine the economic policies of the British government. Your first priority is the voters, and this policy helps them. No cost. Now turn to p. 92.

OFFICIAL – SENSITIVE

YOU REVERSE THE VAT CUT

You're back in the House of Commons the very next afternoon to give an emergency statement, rows of braying and mocking opposition MPs waving their white order papers at you like flags of surrender.

'This government has an iron-clad commitment to financial and economic stability,' you say over the din, and hence you have decided to reverse the VAT cut. Where there were cheers and delight on the benches behind you at the Spring Statement, there's now a painful silence. The prime minister is also conspicuously absent, happy to let you face this humiliation alone.

'Mr Speaker, I think we can all draw a simple conclusion from the chancellor's U-turn today,' your chief political opponent, the shadow chancellor, says in reply to your statement. 'That this government is *woefully incompetent, inept* and *economically illiterate*. And a general election can't come soon enough!'

Your fellow MPs avoid making eye contact with you as you leave the chamber and you take refuge in your parliamentary office, dreading the extensive round of media interviews you'll now have to do defending the decision. Polly is sullen but June is more upbeat as she opens the Bloomberg app on her phone.

'It worked,' she says. 'Gilts rallying. We stopped the rot.'

You spend the rest of the afternoon fielding questions from journalists on whether you need to resign and whether you continue to have the backing of the prime minister.

'Of course I do,' you say, feigning an assurance you don't feel.

No. 10 eventually issues a statement of their own, saying the PM has full confidence in you.

'Even if the chancellor's VAT plan may have been misguided, the PM can't think of a better person for the job,' an ally of the prime minister is quoted as saying in *The Times*.

Polly is furious – 'The chancellor's VAT plan! The absolute cheek of No. 10!' – and says she'll start a counterbriefing. You tell her to stand down – you don't want relations to become any more awkward with your boss.

The fallout from your U-turn dominates the media for the next week, with endless column inches dedicated to the question of your future and commentators openly speculating about who might replace you. Polly is stoic throughout, giving you pep talks about how you've achieved the most important and under-appreciated outcome in politics: survival.

Deduct eight points from your approval rating.

It's now time to check your political score.
If your approval rating is 0 or in the negative,
turn to p. 97. If it's more than 0, turn to p. 95.

YOU KEEP THE VAT CUT

On the third day of market pain – your borrowing costs are still rising, the pound is sinking, June's fingernails have been bitten to shreds – you get a call from the Governor of the Bank of England. He informs you that the central bank is preparing an emergency intervention to stabilise the situation.

'Though I fear our action alone won't be enough,' he says. 'You may wish to … reconsider your fiscal plans.'

On the fifth day of market pain – the Bank's mass buying up of UK government bonds does stem the slide initially, but a fresh sell-off takes hold as you continue to defend the tax cut – you meet an ashen-faced prime minister in No. 10. On her desk, there's a spread of the newspapers which have been fully seized of the market crisis for the past few days, documenting all the pain for the public: higher mortgage costs causing house purchases to collapse, holidays rendered unaffordable by the sinking pound, the expected hit to the cost of living because imported goods are now more expensive due to the weakened currency, and so on.

'Maybe we have to U-turn after all,' she says, her voice hollow. You concede that yes, the moment has perhaps come. But what she says next is chilling.

'It can't be you,' she says, not looking you in the eye. 'It has to be a fresh face. You have to take the fall for all of this. I'm sorry.'

You feel unsteady on your feet as you process what the prime minister is saying. You are being fired. You begin to defend yourself but the prime minister holds up a hand.

'It's decided,' she says. 'I accept your resignation.'

You walk in a daze back to your study in No. 11, bracing for the ignominy of the next few days: the unflattering picture of your gloomy face that they'll plaster across the front pages, the sad farewell to your Treasury officials and aides, the political obituaries they will write about the humiliating end to your career. And all so that you can be the scapegoat for the prime minister and the tax cut that she so badly wanted. It leaves a bitter taste in the mouth.

Commiserations! Your journey as chancellor has come to an end. Return to p. 78 to try again!

YOUR SURPLUS IS POSITIVE
AFTER CUTTING VAT

The next day's papers couldn't be better. It's wall-to-wall praise of the VAT cut and you're the hero of the hour. The tabloids are jubilant, declaring you a political mastermind who's given your party a vital pre-election boost.

'Have a Load of VAT!' screams the *Sun*. 'VAT a Gift, Chancellor!' says the *Daily Star*.

The only words of criticism come on the inside pages of the *Financial Times*, which notes that you've taken a hammer to your headroom to fund this tax giveaway.

'*A chancellor's desire to be popular in the run-up to a general election is natural*', the paper's leader column admits. '*But they mustn't lose sight of their fundamental duty to be prudent with the public finances. What the chancellor announced yesterday amounted to throwing caution to the wind.*'

'Oh boo to them,' Polly says in your study. 'There's no pleasing the FT.'

'They do have a point, though,' June says. 'We're running things pretty tight.'

It's now time to check your political score.

If your approval rating is 0 or in the negative, turn to p. 97. If it's more than 0, turn to p. 95.

YOUR POLITICAL APPROVAL
RATING IS POSITIVE

You're breathing a sigh of relief on making it past your first major milestone as chancellor when Polly enters your study in No. 11, a copy of that week's *Economist* in hand.

'You'll enjoy this,' she says.

STEADY AS SHE GOES

Britain's chancellor is walking the political tightrope with aplomb

It's a feat achieved by very few in politics, but it's one being carried off by Britain's chancellor nevertheless: a net favourable approval rating with the public, even as they exercise the tricky and heavy burden of power. It's a feat made all the more remarkable by the fragility in Britain's public finances, a fragility the chancellor will certainly be wary of. But for now, credit where credit is due. Popular chancellors are few and far between, and yet we have one now in the Treasury.

Polly unveils two whisky tumblers and sets them on your desk, glugging out generous measures for you both. She proposes a toast.

'To merriment, prosperity and your universal reign in the Treasury,' she says, downing her drink. 'Until you become prime minister, naturally.'

She then inspects her glass and says: 'So. What are you going to drink on Budget Day?'

You admit that your choice of beverage a few months from now has been low on your list of priorities, but it is indeed an interesting question. By historic parliamentary tradition, the chancellor is allowed a tipple at the despatch box when delivering their Budget, the only occasion when alcohol is allowed in the House of Commons chamber. An impressive assortment of drinks has been consumed down the years – Gladstone: sherry with beaten egg; Disraeli: brandy with water; Howe: gin and tonic – and you say you'll have to give it some thought.

'I say three shots of sambuca,' Polly says. 'That'll get the old synapses firing. Really give 'em a Budget to remember.'

You thank Polly for her advice and say you look forward to the day when it is in fact her running the nation's finances.

Now turn to p. 99.

YOUR APPROVAL RATING IS NEGATIVE

You're feeling relieved at having made it past your first major milestone as chancellor when Polly enters your study in No. 11 Downing Street, a copy of that week's *Spectator* tucked under her arm. The cover shows you teetering on a tightrope, with the headline: 'Britain's Wobbling Chancellor'.

'I'll give them wobbling,' Polly says. 'No Christmas card for the Speccy this year.'

You nevertheless take the magazine with interest and begin to read.

It's a golden rule of politics: the Chancellor of the Exchequer will always, at some point, become unpopular. But even this government must be alarmed at the haste with which the chancellor has fallen from public favour. Having arrived with such steady approval ratings just a few months ago, our finance minister has much to do to get back on track. And in an election year, the stakes couldn't be higher. No prime minister wants to go to the country with the albatross of an unpopular chancellor around their neck. Such baggage may be the difference between victory and defeat in the tight race forecast by the polls. So, as our Treasury minister wobbles on the tightrope of political survival, surely the nudging hand of No. 10 cannot be far away.

'What nonsense,' Polly says. 'Don't believe a word of it.'

You thank Polly for her support but you're less blasé. You've seen what's happened to public sentiment towards you and it's making you nervous. You also know how ruthless the prime minister can be. Polly spies your apprehension and unfurls two whisky tumblers, pouring generous measures for you both.

'Chin up, chancellor,' she says, raising her glass. 'We're doing just fine. There's no chance the PM will fire you. Not this close to an election. And you've still got the Budget to come. It's all to play for. Speaking of which.' Polly inspects her glass. 'What are you going to drink on the big day?'

Your choice of refreshment months from now is certainly far from your mind, but it's an interesting and quirky question. By parliamentary convention, the chancellor is allowed to consume an alcoholic drink while delivering the Budget speech, the only time that alcohol is allowed in the House of Commons chamber. You say you'll have to give it some thought.

'Just don't pick something weird,' Polly says, who then pulls various faces as she lists tipples of chancellors past. Gladstone's sherry with beaten egg? Awful. Disraeli's brandy with water? Who needs the water? Dalton's rum and milk? Now we're talking.

'I think I'd pick straight vodka,' she says. 'Go hard or go home.'

You thank Polly for her advice but, on that particular point, you say you may have to demure.

Now turn to p. 99.

PART 2

Events,
Dear Boy,
Events

Unexpected things can happen.
Problems can arise.

Norman Lamont

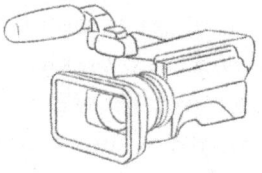

CHAPTER 12

The Announcement

You've got to deal with the
psychology of the people in power.
Kwasi Kwarteng

The Treasury marches to the drumbeat of fiscal events, and
the ink is barely dry on your Spring Statement when you're
already being invited to preparatory meetings for the next
one, the biggie: the Budget. Sir Alex tells you that it may
be several months away, but that time will pass in a flash.
You're just about to enter one of those initial Budget meetings with him when Polly pulls you to one side and says she
has fantastic news.

'Clear the schedule, chancellor,' she says. 'Epic photo
opportunity incoming.'

She tells you that one of the world's biggest tech companies at the cutting edge of artificial intelligence has decided
to relocate its main headquarters to London, bringing with
them thousands of new jobs and billions in new investment.
Polly says it's a huge vote of confidence in your chancellorship
and the work of this government, a gift from above ahead of
the election. And, best of all, the company wants you to make

the announcement in just a few days' time at the site where they're planning to construct a billion-pound hi-tech hub.

'I'll tell No. 10; we'll get it top of the grid,' she says, referring to the government's weekly communication plan managed by Downing Street. 'How exciting!'

But when you exit your Budget meeting an hour later you find Polly's mood has completely turned, and she asks to speak with you in private. She says she has a disappointing update: the prime minister is demanding that she makes the announcement in your place.

'I think she's jealous,' Polly says. 'What with being upstaged and all.'

You think upstaged is a bit of an exaggeration, but it's definitely been a quirk of the last few months. Despite the intensity and challenges of your stint in the Treasury so far, your approval ratings have consistently outstripped those of the prime minister. It's perhaps to be expected given that she's been in post for far longer than you and you hadn't given it much thought, but now you wonder whether your relative popularity might indeed be a point of envy.

'As a point of principle, chancellor, I really think we should tell No. 10 where to go,' Polly says. 'You're the chancellor. This announcement is squarely about the economy. You're running the economy. It's not like we go round demanding to make policy announcements willy-nilly on their patch. We should be firm.'

Polly's thumbs are hovering over her phone, ready to reply to No. 10. She asks what she should say.

It's time to make your next decision.

DECISION

Reject No. 10's request. You agree with Polly that it should be for the chancellor to announce news like this. The prime minister is trying to steal your limelight and you want to show No. 10 that you can't just be pushed around. What's more, you're sure this photo op will be great for your personal brand and approval ratings. It's not fair for No. 10 to try to take that away from you. If you choose this option, turn to p. 104.

Accept No. 10's request. You disagree with Polly. While you'd like to make this announcement, you respect the prime minister's authority and want to maintain positive relations with No. 10. In any event, what's most important is how the public views your political party ahead of the election, so it doesn't matter whether it's you or the prime minister announcing this news. If you choose this option, turn to p. 112.

OFFICIAL – SENSITIVE

YOU REJECT NO. 10'S REQUEST

Polly fires off the message but there is no reply from No. 10. Later that evening, just as you're finishing dinner in your flat above No. 11, you get a message from the prime minister: 'Can we chat?'

It's a curiosity of running the country that your chief political colleague and line manager also happens to live in the same building as you, so you walk through the Downing Street house in your slippers to the No. 10 flat. The flat is actually smaller than yours, hence why prime ministers past such as Tony Blair and David Cameron took the No. 11 accommodation for themselves and their families, but this prime minister said she preferred the idea of living in No. 10. ('The postal address is cooler,' she'd said with a wink.) You find Emily sipping red wine in the kitchen wearing a baggy T-shirt and grey sweatpants, the casual, private image the public never gets to see. You notice that the bottle at her side is three-quarters drained. She offers you a drink but you refuse.

'How's everything going?' she asks. You exchange pleasantries that quickly become an awkward silence, the reason for your meeting obvious.

'I've got to say, I was surprised at the pushback today,' she says eventually, looking into her drink. 'Always had you down as a team player.'

You begin to defend yourself but Emily raises her hand.

'It's okay, I get it,' she says. 'We're all politicians. But. You know. Who's First Lord of the Treasury?' She laughs and sips her wine. 'Only kidding. But also. Not really.'

She sets down her glass and gives you a look. The silence lengthens. It's clear she expects you to speak next. It's time to make your next decision.

DECISION

Stand your ground. You understand the prime minister's disappointment, but your reasoning and the point of principle remain. Major economic announcements are the purview of the chancellor, and she shouldn't be allowed to swoop in and steal your thunder. If you choose this option, turn to p. 108.

OFFICIAL – SENSITIVE

DECISION

Back down. You've made your point with No. 10, but now you think it's best to give the prime minister what she wants. She is your boss after all, and clearly this is important to her. It'll be a shame to miss out on the publicity of the announcement, but sometimes you have to pick your battles. If you choose this option, turn to p. 112.

OFFICIAL – SENSITIVE

YOU STAND YOUR GROUND

The prime minister hears you out with a frown. She pours herself another glass when you finish.

'Sure,' she says. 'I just thought you'd see it differently.'

A few days later, you're standing before an array of television cameras at a building site in east London, feeling very glad you put your foot down with the prime minister. The tech company's executive team are standing alongside you as you announce the investment, which you say marks a fantastic day for Britain. The company's CEO steps forward and shakes your hand, a pose you hold for the snappers. You spot Polly off to the side, her expression like that of a child on Christmas morning.

'We'd particularly like to thank the chancellor for all the support so far,' the CEO says. 'We can't wait to get started.'

Polly is so pleased with the ensuing press coverage that she frames the front page of the next day's *Telegraph*, which features a huge photo of your grip-and-grin with the CEO and the caption 'Chancellor seals the deal'. Polly says she reckons fighting No. 10 is the best piece of advice she's ever given you.

'Just remember that when you're dishing out the plum jobs when you're prime minister,' she says. 'You know. Ambassador to St Lucia. Special envoy to the Bahamas.'

Add three points to your approval rating.

You return to your Budget planning in the weeks after the big corporate announcement and have all but put the disagreement with the prime minister out of your head until the arrival of a strange Wednesday morning. Wednesdays mark the peak of political activity and energy in Westminster, centred on the famous Prime Minister's Questions (PMQs) at noon, and you're making your way over to Parliament when Polly reads from her phone with surprise.

'This is strange,' she says. 'Lots of rumours about a Cabinet reshuffle.'

You agree: that would be very strange indeed. A Cabinet reshuffle – where the prime minister shakes up the personnel in the top jobs in government – is something you would have expected to have had some input on as the second-most senior minister. Or, at the very least, you should've been told one was coming. But this news hits you completely cold. Polly says it's probably just the typical Westminster rumour mill, but she'll message some people in No. 10 to check.

Your ministerial car completes the short journey between the Treasury and Parliament – ministers in yesteryear might have simply walked, but you use the Jaguar for security reasons – and you make your way to the Commons for PMQs. Polly tells you that No. 10 are ignoring her, but they're probably just busy. The prime minister arrives to typical hearty cheers from the backbenches and takes her seat beside you, though she greets you with an unusual stiffness and formality.

Over the course of the next half-hour, as the prime minister bobs up and down answering questions and you try to keep a straight face for the cameras, your sliver of doubt morphs into a full-blown paranoia, your mind jumping to various worrying conclusions. A pre-election reshuffle might make sense, you reason, so that the prime minister can put all her favourite people in the key positions for the election campaign, a chance to axe any dead weights who won't bring in votes. Her favourite people … does that include you, though? You're also thinking about the conversation you had in the No. 10 flat. Surely she doesn't still hold that against you, does she? You're desperate for PMQs to end so that you can speak to her, but she briskly leaves after the final question and you get a tap on the shoulder from one of her parliamentary bag-carriers.

'Chancellor,' the MP whispers. 'The PM would like to see you in her office. Right now.'

And that's when your heart falls. Because in all your time as chancellor, never once have you had a formal meeting with the prime minister in her House of Commons office, located just next to yours behind the Speaker's Chair. You've always met somewhere in Downing Street. The PM's parliamentary office is famously a site of political executions, the place where firings are conducted during a Cabinet reshuffle to spare ministers the humiliation of having to trudge up the street to No. 10 in full view of the world's media just before they get sacked. You enter with trepidation.

'I'd like you to become a junior minister in the environment department,' the prime minister says, without any other greeting or introduction. 'You'd be the perfect fit.'

You can't quite believe what's happening. This is a brutal demotion, the political equivalent of a seafarer being asked to walk the plank. The prime minister is watching your face and you think you see a glint of revenge. You knew she could be ruthless, but this is something else. You're reminded of Polly's favourite political parable from Herodotus, of the Athenian general who'd cut off the tallest ears in a grain field, a demonstration of how to retain power. Perhaps you'd grown too tall in the wheat field of Westminster, become too much of a popular threat to her. Or maybe she was just being vindictive. The hollow words sound like they're coming from someone else, but they're your own: you say that you accept, seeing no alternative.

'Brilliant,' the prime minister says. 'Like I said. Always knew you were a team player.'

You slump into your ministerial car back to the Treasury and break the news to Polly. She's livid. You tune out her venting and brace for the ignominy of the next few days: the unflattering picture of your gloomy face that they'll plaster across the front pages, the sad farewell to your Treasury officials and aides, the political obituaries they will write about this humiliating downfall. Quite frankly, you're stunned.

Commiserations! Your time as chancellor has come to an end. Return to p. 101 to try again!

YOU'VE LET NO. 10 MAKE
THE ANNOUNCEMENT

The prime minister is very grateful and so, a few days later, you're standing on the sidelines at a building site in east London watching her make the announcement, surrounded by a beaming executive team and an array of television cameras. The prime minister says this is a fantastic vote of confidence in Britain and will create thousands of new jobs. The company's CEO steps forward and shakes her hand, a pose they hold for the photographers.

'This should be you,' Polly whispers through gritted teeth.

Polly's mood worsens in the aftermath when she sees the fawning coverage in the newspapers and the poll boost received by the prime minister, the picture of the PM's grip-and-grin making a clean sweep of the front pages, the favoured caption being 'PM seals the deal'.

'She literally didn't though!' Polly says. 'We did. I really think you should stand up for yourself more, chancellor. We can't always let No. 10 get their way. This was a big opportunity missed.'

Now turn to p. 113.

CHAPTER 13

Off to America

As Chancellors frequently discover,
the rosy hues of dawn often give way
to overcast skies by mid-morning.
James Callaghan, Chancellor of the Exchequer, 1964–7

One of the perks of being chancellor – a welcome break from the strains of the Budget and the intensity of domestic scrutiny – is the opportunity for international travel, and you happen to have an important visit on the horizon: to Britain's largest single-country trading partner and historic ally, the United States. The visit is all the more important because of a long-mooted-yet-finally-in-sight prospect – that of a comprehensive free-trade deal between the two nations. A fully fledged accord with the US has been touted as a major prospective benefit since Britain left the European Union in 2020, and you've inherited a situation where the stars are aligning.

'Scope out the Americans,' the prime minister tells you, as you chat in the famous garden of 10 Downing Street in the days before your trip. 'I'll admit, I'm still undecided. There's a reason why it's taken so long to get this deal over the line.'

You're reviewing the itinerary of the US trip with Sir Alex when Polly and June join you in your office in the Treasury. Polly is complaining that you're all flying commercial to the US and asks why you couldn't take the prime minister's private RAF plane, the Airbus Voyager with its golden 'United Kingdom' lettering and impressive Union Jack tail.

'I'm afraid that use of the prime minister's jet for ministerial visits is managed by the Ministry of Defence [MOD],' Sir Alex says, looking over his spectacles. 'And given that we in the Treasury have kept a vice-like grip on the MOD's budget for many years, their response has been to frequently make the aircraft mysteriously unavailable to the chancellor. A bit of retaliatory guerrilla Whitehall warfare, if you will.'

June hands you a full briefing dossier to prepare you for meeting your US counterpart – the Treasury secretary – and reminds you of the next day's GDP figures. You'd almost forgotten: part of the job of chancellor is responding to a seemingly endless slew of economic data – inflation numbers, consumer confidence, government borrowing levels – and you'd lost track that it's already time for the next GDP update.

'I fear this one won't be so good,' she says.

And it's that GDP update which is on your mind as you board your flight to Washington, an unwelcome setback which is a reminder of the vulnerability of your economic position. The ONS has announced GDP growth came in weaker than forecast in the last quarter, with the impact of the Bank's interest rate hike rippling through the economy. Higher borrowing costs meant less spending by households, as they faced higher mortgage payments. It also meant less investment by companies, as loans they might have taken to spend on new machinery or projects became too expensive.

'Well let's just hope our good old friends the Yanks have some better news,' Polly says, quaffing her complimentary post-takeoff gin and tonic and trying to raise your spirits.

Deduct £2 billion from your surplus.
Now turn to p. 116.

CHAPTER 14

The US Trade Deal

I'm a very strong believer in free trade....
Self-sufficiency isn't a good aim.
Norman Lamont

You take the chance while cruising at 36,000 feet over the Atlantic Ocean to read June's dossier on the US visit, taking a keen interest in the latest on the trade deal. Signing new free-trade agreements – FTAs, as they're called – has been a priority of the British government since Brexit, a bid to counterbalance the new barriers to commerce that arose with the EU after the split, but you share the uncertainty of the prime minister. While you sense signing an agreement with the US would be an eye-catching symbolic moment for the government, you're also wary of any potential backlash and want to be sure that the economic gains will be worth it. Helpfully, June has created a list of pros and cons, which you read now.

PROS	CONS
• **Cheaper goods for UK consumers and businesses.** An FTA would remove tariffs on imports from the US, meaning households and firms could buy products like electronic goods, cars and machinery more cheaply from America.	• **Potential backlash.** The US is known to aggressively advocate for its key economic interests in trade talks, including liberalising access for its agricultural products. The US has weaker health and safety regulations in areas such as food, meaning we may have to accept chlorine-washed chicken and hormone-fed beef coming into Britain as part of the deal. This is likely to spark a backlash among our farmers, who will fear being undercut.
• **More commercial opportunities for British firms.** An FTA would remove tariffs on exports from Britain to the US, meaning sellers of products like Cheddar cheese, ceramics, Scottish salmon and Scotch whisky could boost their sales into the world's largest economy.	• **Pressure on NHS drug prices.** Another US interest in trade talks is to boost its pharmaceuticals sector, and it would like to increase the prices their drugs can command in the NHS. The US may make this a condition of the deal, but it would be an extra burden on the NHS's budget.
• *Major PR Victory.* (*You notice this bullet has been hastily added in Polly's handwriting.*) *Prospect of a big fancy photo op in the White House and your name in the history books, plus likely emphatic reception across much of the British media.*	• **Limited economic impact.** The latest official assessment of a deal by the UK government found it would only boost GDP by 0.16 per cent in 15 years. It's therefore unlikely that the OBR would give you any meaningful upgrade to your surplus in the near term.

You're still mulling the trade deal when you're making your way towards the US Treasury building in DC, Polly playing the role of unashamed tourist as you approach: goggling at the grandeur of the dome of the US Capitol building; admiring the tranquillity of the Lincoln Memorial Reflecting Pool; neck craning at the Washington Monument. You're passed by a gentleman wearing a red T-shirt with Donald Trump's popular slogan: 'Make America Great Again'.

'I think we should actually Make America Great Britain Again,' Polly says, now looking up at the impressive neoclassical exterior of the US Treasury, before which stands a statue of Alexander Hamilton, the first Treasury secretary.

'For the sake of the special relationship, please never say that again,' June says.

You come away from the meeting – held in the secretary's illustrious conference room, lit by nineteenth-century gas chandeliers and overlooked by a portrait of founding father George Washington – with two key takeaways. The first is that the trade deal is very advanced indeed, to the point of only needing final sign-off by your respective national leaders. And the shape of the deal is much as described by June's briefing note: a reduction in tariffs on UK–US trade that would help British firms and households, but also concessions to the US on access to the UK market for their agricultural goods and pharmaceutical products.

The second is that the US is increasingly concerned by recent developments in the Middle East, specifically rising tensions between Iran and Israel on which you'd also been receiving regular updates. The Iranian-backed militia Hezbollah has been launching missile attacks on Israel from Lebanon, and Israel has been responding in turn with strikes on Iran. Your meeting with the Treasury secretary covered how you might protect your respective countries from any economic fallout that might arise from a deepening conflict in the region, and you agreed to keep in touch.

'So it's decision time,' the prime minister says to you in her study in 10 Downing Street, when you return to London and brief her on the discussions. You can see that she's still unsure on the US trade deal, vacillating between being in favour and then against. You sense that your verdict will be decisive. She asks: 'If it were you, chancellor, what would you do?'

It's time to make your next decision.

DECISION

Support the free-trade deal with the US. You think it would be an historic achievement to strike such a deal with one of the UK's most important allies and it would help both British consumers and businesses. And even if the economic gains may be modest and take time, they're still worth having. You also expect it would get a great write-up in a majority of the press, which would give a nice pre-election popularity bump. If you choose this option, turn to p. 122.

OFFICIAL – SENSITIVE

DECISION

Oppose the free-trade deal with the US.
You like the idea of an FTA in principle, but think this deal isn't worth having. You think the concessions to the US go too far and are likely to cause a public blowback. You also worry about the limited economic benefits of an agreement and how you won't reap any budgetary reward this side of the election.
If you choose this option, turn to p. 124.

OFFICIAL – SENSITIVE

YOU SUPPORT THE FREE-TRADE DEAL

Within weeks you're flying back to DC, and this time it certainly is on the prime minister's plane, along with a sizable contingent of reporters. The signing of the trade deal is a moment of great pomp and ceremony in the Oval Office of the White House, with you standing alongside the prime minister as she shares a famous handshake with the president.

'One for the mantelpiece,' Polly says, handing you the front page of the next day's *Times*. The paper hails the trade deal as an important milestone in UK–US relations and a welcome opportunity to deepen economic ties between two great nations. '*Churchill and Roosevelt would be proud,*' it concludes.

But while there's an initial glow of good feeling around the deal, something worrying happens in the days following. It begins with Britain's farming lobby, which is outraged by the provisions on chlorine-washed chicken and hormone-treated beef and organises protests in Westminster. Soon you have a procession of tractors rolling up Whitehall as far as the eye can see, blaring their horns and urging you to ditch the deal in the name of food safety and protecting British farms.

Then the left-wing press starts whipping up a frenzy about the NHS having to pay higher prices for US drugs, and they accuse the government of selling out a national treasure. This also sparks protests, and before long you have both farmers and Britain's medical community camped out in Parliament Square, showering you with choice words and acrimony. Your government tries to sell the benefits of the deal – cheaper goods for consumers and firms, more export opportunities for UK companies – but this gets drowned out by the spectacle of the colourful protests.

'That's the thing about trade deals,' Sir Alex says, as your ministerial car snakes through the angry crowds towards the Treasury after you'd appeared at a parliamentary committee together to defend the FTA. 'They tend to benefit lots of people in a little way – goods slightly cheaper for everyone, for example – but that's not going to draw adoring crowds. Yet they also tend to hurt specific groups of people – like these farmers – a lot. And that will definitely attract the mob.'

You've just seen the latest hit you've taken in the polls because of the backlash against the trade deal when June sticks her head around your office door with more bad news. She informs you that her prediction was correct: the OBR say they won't be upgrading your economic position due to the deal, because its impact is too small.

'The deal will obviously do some good in the long-run,' she says. 'But as a famous economist once said, in the long-run we're all dead.'

Deduct one point from your approval rating.
Now turn to p. 126.

YOU OPPOSE THE FREE-TRADE DEAL

You express your reservations and the prime minister nods in solemn agreement. 'Maybe it's one for our next term in power,' she says, eyes twinkling.

At first, there's lots of media disappointment when they hear the deal is off, and your political opponents attack you for missing an opportunity to remove trade barriers with an economic superpower. Polly is also downbeat – she desperately wanted that tour of the White House – but she spies an opportunity in the days following.

With your permission, she leaks the most controversial sections of the draft trade deal concerning US food imports and drug pricing to friendly journalists in the media, who in turn write stories of a principled chancellor who faced down a deal that ultimately didn't serve Britain's interests. The UK's farming lobby and medical community are ecstatic and you're singled out for praise.

'Chancellor Blocks US FTA over Chlorinated Chicken Fears,' writes the *Guardian*.

'NHS Saved from Higher Drug Prices after Chancellor Stops US FTA,' writes the *Daily Mirror*.

'Chancellor Intervened on US FTA over NHS, Food Red Lines,' declares the *Financial Times*.

'This is actually quite impressive,' June says, surveying the newspaper cuttings.

'Call me Deep Throat,' Polly says. 'With a touch of Malcolm Tucker. I had to shout at the *Mirror* when they didn't initially put "chancellor" in the headline.'

Add one point to your approval rating.
Now turn to p. 126.

CHAPTER 15

A Brewing Crisis

One felt like someone under fire in a battle.
You just had to deal with it.
Norman Lamont on Britain's currency crisis in September 1992

You're keen to get back to Budget planning and the domestic agenda but international affairs continue to dominate in the ensuing weeks, particularly the deteriorating situation in the Middle East. You wake to fresh images each morning of missile strikes on both Tehran and Tel Aviv, the death toll ticking grimly higher. The foreign secretary gives an update at your next Cabinet meeting and describes an increasingly regional conflict that shows little sign of abating. Most worrying for you, Iranian-backed Houthi rebels have started attacking oil sites controlled by Saudi Arabia in retaliation for Saudi support for Israel, and the price of oil is surging.

'Chancellor, what does this mean for us?' the prime minister asks, surveying the gloomy looks around the table.

You explain that you're monitoring energy prices closely, but that we can expect pain for the public. Filling up a car with petrol and heating a home are both about to become a lot more expensive. Goods in the shops will also become dearer because energy is a key input in production, and companies are likely to pass on those higher costs to consumers. We can also expect the Bank of England to increase interest rates again, in an attempt to keep a lid on inflation. You tell your colleagues that the Treasury is drawing up contingency plans to address all of this, but difficult choices lie ahead for the government.

The prime minister asks to speak to you alone when the meeting ends. For all her usual confidence and swagger, you can see she is genuinely worried. You talk through the options your civil servants have been preparing – a major support package funded by tax increases and spending cuts, a major support package funded by government borrowing alone, or doing nothing and hoping the situation improves – and you sense her indecision. 'None of those options sound very appealing,' she says. She asks you to keep a close eye on the situation and be ready to act if needed.

As the press reports get darker by the day – long queues forming at petrol stations, vulnerable pensioners having to choose between heating and eating, a clamour growing for the government to act – the tension rises in the Treasury. Your officials work overtime refining the different options for intervention, and this is the detailed memo they give you as you're weighing your decision.

Option #1 – Major Support Package Funded by Tax Increases and Spending Cuts. A £20 billion intervention to give households a significant discount on their energy bills, insulating them from most of the recent price hike. It would also include a temporary cut to fuel duty – a tax paid at the petrol pumps and on heating fuel. To pay for the package, the government would increase the following taxes:

- **Corporation tax** – a tax on company profits – from 25 per cent to 27 per cent (raising £7 billion)
- **Employers' National Insurance** – a payroll tax paid by firms – from 15 per cent to 16 per cent (raising £10 billion)
- The higher rate of **capital gains tax** – a tax paid on the profit from selling an asset – from 20 per cent to 30 per cent (£500 million)

The government would also find efficiency savings of £2.5 billion in departmental budgets. The Treasury's economists expect this option would have a modest negative effect on the government's surplus because, although the package would be covered by tax and spending decisions, the tax hikes may suppress economic activity.

Option #2 – Major Support Package Funded by Government Borrowing. The same £20 billion intervention as in option 1, yet funding the package entirely through an increase in government borrowing. This option has the merits of requiring no changes to tax or spending policy. Its effect would be to deduct £20 billion from the government's surplus and would require a suspension of the fiscal rules.

Option #3 – Take No Action, Continue to Monitor Events. Given the significant cost implications of options 1 and 2, the government should also consider the merits of non-intervention. The tax increases of option 1 will likely hamper the economy, because they will hit businesses already struggling with higher energy costs. And the borrowing of option 2 will add to Britain's significant debt pile and may risk a negative reaction on financial markets. While likely to be unpopular politically, non-intervention would be best for the government finances.

Fierce debate rages in your office about what to do. June is the biggest proponent of option 1, arguing that doing nothing is becoming untenable and the responsible choice is to offer support while still balancing the books. She says increasing taxes on corporate Britain is regrettable because it will likely hurt economic growth, but it's a necessary evil. Trimming public spending will also be unpopular, she concedes, but the sums need to add up. She's also worried about how investors would react to a major borrowing spree and says the fiscal rules must be sacrosanct.

Option 2's biggest advocate is Polly. She uses a colourful word beginning with 'f' to describe what the government should do to the fiscal rules.

'We're in a crisis!' she says. 'Obviously the normal rules don't apply. The nation's credit card is there for emergencies, and clearly that's what this is. We're already up to our eyeballs in taxes; we can't be jacking them up even more. And don't get me started on spending cuts. The press will spin this as a return to austerity. No. This should definitely come from borrowing.'

Option 3 has its own vocal supporter in the form of your deputy, the Chief Secretary to the Treasury, a man named Simon Miser. A fellow minister in the Cabinet, Simon's responsibilities include running the government's spending review, the often-acrimonious process of setting each department's individual budget. Whenever an opportunity arises for the Treasury to be thrifty and say 'no' to a spending request, Simon will seize it. ('Miser by name, miser by nature,' Polly likes to whisper, whenever he leaves the room.)

Another benefit of having Simon is that he can stand in for you in the House of Commons whenever the opposition try to haul you there to answer a so-called Urgent Question, often a tricky appearance on the thorny issue of the day. He does that for you here, facing down rows of baying MPs – 'Where's the chancellor? When is the government going to act? How much longer must our constituents suffer?' – by calmly and stoically repeating that the Treasury is considering all options and nothing is off the table.

But matters come to a head. The prime minister calls you into her study after another bleak set of front pages and says the time has come to choose. Here's your next decision.

DECISION

Announce the support package funded by tax increases and spending cuts. You agree with June. You want to help with the soaring cost of living but also want to retain your reputation for fiscal prudence. You dislike the idea of higher taxes and slimming public services, but you dislike the alternatives even more. *Deduct £3 billion from your surplus.* If you choose this option, turn to p. 134.

Announce the support package funded by government borrowing. You agree with Polly. Special times call for special measures, and it's reasonable to suspend the fiscal rules while you combat this crisis. Investors will see that this is only temporary, so there's limited risk of any major blowback on markets. *Deduct £20 billion from your surplus.* If you choose this option, turn to p. 136.

OFFICIAL – SENSITIVE

DECISION

Take no action; continue to monitor events.
You agree with Simon. The best bet for your financial position would be to take a step back. You don't want to hurt the economy with tax increases and you don't want to risk loading up the nation's credit card. It'll mean disappointing the voters, but sometimes as chancellor you just have to say no. If you choose this option, turn to p. 147.

OFFICIAL – SENSITIVE

YOU ANNOUNCE THE SUPPORT
PACKAGE FUNDED BY TAX
INCREASES AND SPENDING CUTS

You enter a packed House of Commons amid a buzz of anticipation. Emergency fiscal statements are a rare thing, and you're about to deliver one now. You feel the pressure of this moment, knowing how much rides on getting it right. Above you, to your left, are the representatives of the fourth estate, the collection of assembled journalists and sketch writers in the Press Gallery from whom most of the country will get their impression of what you're about to announce. Pens are poised.

The generosity of the support package gets a reassuringly loud cheer from your backbenchers, but there's also awkward shuffling of order papers and coughing when you spell out the tax increases and spending cuts. Your MPs know this is painful. The mood is sombre when you take your seat, your concluding remarks met with a muted 'hear hear'. Then it's the anxious wait for how it lands.

As you sit in your study in No. 11 that evening, survey-ing the early editions of the front pages with Polly, you feel cautious relief. The consensus is that your intervention will take the sting out of a lot of the cost-of-living pain being felt in the country, but there are still hard times in store. The right-wing press dislikes your tax hikes and say you're piling further misery on companies that they can ill afford. But your overriding sense is that it could've been a lot worse.

The first polls in the days after still show a hefty hit to your popularity – no-one much likes the government when their bills are going up, and you've become the public face of this crisis – yet Polly is still chipper.

'As damage limitation goes, chancellor, I don't think we could've done much more,' she says.

Deduct five points from your approval rating.
Now turn to p. 153.

YOU CHOOSE THE SUPPORT PACKAGE
FUNDED BY GOVERNMENT BORROWING

The House of Commons is a tense hush as you stand to announce the package. Emergency fiscal statements are a rare thing in British politics and much of your speech is received in sombre silence, your fellow MPs recognising the gravity of the situation and the pain being felt by the public. You get the occasional heckle – 'Why's it taken so long, chancellor? What were you waiting for?' – but you're buoyed by the healthy cheers that greet the generosity of the intervention. You notice some quizzical looks on the opposition benches when you explain how the giveaway will be funded, but the initial response from your party is loud approval.

Then it's the turn of the shadow chancellor. After criticising your delay in announcing help for the public, they attack your suspension of the fiscal rules.

'While we on this side of the House welcome the chancellor's decision to finally act, we have serious misgivings about this borrowing splurge,' they say. 'Sound money is the bedrock of good government and we don't support piling an enormous burden on future generations who will have to pay this money back.'

Polly is enthusiastically showing you the optimistic first-takes of Britain's chief political commentators as your ministerial car makes the short trip back to the Treasury – 'a *sizable offer*', '*the chancellor has met the measure of this crisis*', '*significant help and not a day too late*' – but June interrupts.

'Markets hate it,' she says. She hands you a live graph on her phone with a line spiking upwards.

'But the line's going up,' Polly says. 'That's good, right?'

'Not when that's our borrowing costs,' she says.

You share a drink with June in the No. 11 flat that evening and you feel uneasy. The market fallout had continued all afternoon, the sell-off only stopped by the end of the trading day at 4.30pm. The rise in borrowing costs already means a significant increase in your debt interest payments and June predicts it's only going to get worse. She advises you to change course to restore Britain's economic credibility. You also receive a call from the Governor of the Bank of England, who informs you the Bank stands ready to intervene to stabilise the situation.

'But I worry we alone can't fix this,' he says. 'It may be necessary to … reconsider your fiscal plans.'

You're at your desk in the Treasury braced for the market opening at 8am the next morning and the rout continues. At 8.07am, Sir Alex pokes his head around the door.

'Chancellor, you may remember I once warned against the dangers of being on an emergency conference call with the DRM team,' he says. 'Alas, your presence is requested on such a call now.'

Your officials do their best to explain what's gone wrong. In a world of international capital flows and globalised financial markets, they say, investors have an expansive choice about where to put their cash. Do they want to lend money to the United States? Or France? Or Britain? Or some other country? Or perhaps they want to put their funds into something else entirely, like gold? Or oil? Or stocks and shares? Investors are making constant judgements about the relative risk and attractiveness of all these different options. And the problem with your borrowing spree and suspension of the fiscal rules is that you've put a big red flag with the word 'risk' on the UK. Whereas you previously had a reputation for caution and prudence, investors now worry that you're profligate and are less likely to pay them back. Hence they're demanding higher and higher rates of return to lend you money.

Your officials explain that the pound is also falling. This is because the UK is now seen as a riskier bet compared to other economies, so investors are putting their money into other currencies, like the US dollar and the Japanese yen. And the falling pound is a problem because it will push up inflation, because it's now more expensive for the UK to import goods from abroad due to its weaker currency, and hence the Bank is more likely to increase interest rates to keep a lid on rising prices. And the expectation of higher interest rates is also a factor pushing up your borrowing costs.

'I don't say this lightly, chancellor,' Sir Alex says. 'But this threatens to become a vicious cycle. We may have to entertain the prospect of a U-turn.'

You call the prime minister but she's blasé. 'Just a bit of turbulence,' she says. She's sure markets will soon correct themselves when people realise this is an emergency, one-off intervention. 'If we're worried about our credibility,' she says, 'then flip-flopping would only make it worse.'

At noon, the Bank of England steps in. The governor issues a press notice saying that the Bank will start buying UK government bonds to address 'the ongoing liquidity issues' in the market. June explains that this is finance-speak for 'Everyone is selling our debt and no-one wants to buy it'.

To Polly's great relief, the Bank's intervention appears to work: your borrowing costs stabilise, albeit at a painfully elevated level. A strange calm descends on the Treasury that afternoon, like that on a battlefield where it's unclear if there's a ceasefire or a permanent peace.

'We're through the worst of it,' Polly says.

'I'm not so sure,' June replies.

That evening, you're scheduled to do a live sit-down interview with the economics editor of the BBC, a booking organised by Polly so that you can explain the merits of your support package to the nation. But instead of honing your talking points on the help for the public, your prep session becomes a spillover of the debate between Polly and June about whether you still need to change course. Polly is adamant that the storm has passed; June says the threat remains. June's view is that you're inevitably going to be asked about the market turmoil in the interview, and this is the moment where you should announce the U-turn. Polly goes increasingly red in the face during June's counsel and calls her advice cowardly and the road to political humiliation. It's time to make your next decision.

DECISION

Announce the U-turn. You agree with June. While markets have stabilised, there's no guarantee this will continue. The safer bet is to change course and announce tax hikes and spending cuts to fund the package. Polly is right: this will be humiliating. But better a humiliation than losing control of the economy. If you choose this option, turn to p. 142.

If you choose this option, turn to p. 142.

OFFICIAL – SENSITIVE

DECISION

Stay the course. You agree with Polly. You've taken a hit on financial markets but the worst has now passed. Your political reputation would never survive such an embarrassing volte-face. It's better to convey confidence to markets and the public. And anyway, you know that hiking taxes and cutting spending would also be unpopular. There's no need to inflict that on the nation. If you choose this option, turn to p. 144.

OFFICIAL – SENSITIVE

YOU ANNOUNCE THE U-TURN

Where there was tension and silence in the House of Commons when you first announced your support package, there is now an expectant glee among your political opponents as you enter the chamber for your second emergency statement. Your cryptic comment in the BBC interview the night before – that you were well aware of what'd been happening on markets, and you'd have more to say about the funding of your intervention in due course – had sparked a frenzied evening of speculation about an imminent U-turn. The opposition MPs are waving their white order papers at you, mocking surrender, while the prime minister is glowering at your side. She'd taken much convincing about the necessity of a change of course, and had said she'd only back you on one condition: that you take the rap for everything.

'This government believes in fiscal responsibility,' you say, struggling to be heard over the jeers and mocking laughter from the green benches opposite. 'And that's why we've reconsidered our approach to the cost-of-living support.'

Polly is glumly reading you the worst of the verdicts in the papers the next morning ('Cowed by the Markets', 'Britain's Out-of-Depth Chancellor', 'Chancellor's Day of Humiliation') when June enters with a smile.

'It's worked,' she says. 'Gilts still rallying.'

Investors welcomed your U-turn and the UK's borrowing costs are once again in retreat. The Bank also announces it is ending its emergency intervention, citing a 'normalisation' in financial conditions. Sir Alex is visibly relieved.

'Mission accomplished,' June says. Polly holds up a newspaper. She says she'd hate to see mission failed.

Add £17 billion to your surplus and deduct five points from your approval rating. Now turn to p. 153.

YOU STAY THE COURSE

The BBC interviewer wastes no time getting to the crunch question.

'You've been reckless and irresponsible with the nation's finances, haven't you?' they say. 'Aren't you embarrassed that the Bank had to step in? You need to change course, don't you, chancellor?'

You take a moment to compose yourself, just as Polly had advised, before calmly explaining that no, you hadn't been reckless at all. You'd simply done what was in the best interests of the long-suffering public, and that emergency times called for emergency measures. The stabilisation in markets that afternoon had fully vindicated your position. You say you have no regrets, none whatsoever.

Polly is giving you the big thumbs-up in your ministerial car on the way back from the studios after and the PM sends you an approving message, but June is watching the passing traffic with eyes glazed.

'I think we got the tone wrong,' she says. '"Fully vindicated" was probably too much.'

You're studying the next day's *Times* cartoon in your office in the Treasury – they've mocked you up like Edith Piaf singing '*Je ne regrette rien*' against a backdrop of traders shouting 'sell!' – when Sir Alex enters without knocking.

'Chancellor, I am very sorry to have to say this,' he says. 'But your presence is *once again* requested on a conference call with DRM.'

To your dismay, the sell-off is back with a vengeance. You're informed that various banks had put out research notes overnight criticising your BBC interview and saying that UK bonds are likely to fall further because of the chancellor's *'cavalier'* approach. You question whether 'cavalier' isn't a bit harsh.

'Maybe,' June says on the call. 'But the bond vigilantes are a sensitive bunch. Often, it's about vibes. And if you give them any excuse ...'

You call the prime minister to update her on the situation, but oddly you can't get through. Her private secretaries tell you she's otherwise engaged in important meetings. 'Are they more important than a developing economic crisis?' you ask. 'Yes,' they say. Apparently so.

Finally, after another brutal session on the markets ends with your borrowing costs at new multi-decade highs, you're told the PM is ready to see you in Downing Street. You find her at her desk in the No. 10 study, her mood subdued and voice hollow.

'I think we got this one wrong,' she says, gaze downcast. 'And it's time to change course.'

She looks into her hands for several moments before meeting your eye.

'It can't be you,' she says. 'I accept your resignation.'

You can't believe what you're hearing. Only 24 hours ago the prime minister was egging you on, saying there was no cause for concern. And now you're being fired. You begin to protest but she holds up her hand.

'I'm sorry,' she says. 'There's no other way.'

You trudge back to your own study in No. 11, your thoughts tumultuous with the indignities that await: the tearful goodbye to your Treasury officials and aides, the sad picture of your face that will dominate the next day's front pages, the political obituaries they'll write about the swift end to your career. You also think about the mundanity of having to pack up your belongings and move out of Downing Street. One moment you're one of the most powerful people in the country. And then, in a single act of cruel dismissal, you're not. Quite simply, you're in shock.

Commiserations! Your journey as chancellor has come to an end. Return to p. 126 to try again!

YOU TAKE NO ACTION;
CONTINUE TO MONITOR EVENTS

Polly comes into work for the next few weeks looking like she's having kittens, her mettle severely tested by your position of non-intervention. The protests around Whitehall get worse and worse, thousands of people marching the streets demanding action on the cost of living, their placards and chants vitriolic towards you and your government. Unperturbed, however, is your deputy, Simon, and he invites you into his office to look at the public finances spreadsheet ahead of the upcoming spending review.

'The numbers are looking great,' he says, speaking over a loudspeaker that is demanding the fall of the government. 'You know what I say. Count the pennies and the pounds look after themselves.'

The negative press coverage is relentless, however, and you're the focus of the criticism. No. 10 sources even start briefing against you, characterising the decision as yours alone, an example of a recalcitrant Treasury holding back an otherwise sympathetic and understanding prime minister. The PM swears the briefings are completely unauthorised and don't reflect her views, but you have serious doubts. The verdict in the papers after a fortnight of all this is that your political reputation has taken a serious beating. It only takes one crisis to turn the public against a chancellor, and that's what's happened here.

If your approval rating is already less than 0, deduct 5 points from your approval rating. Otherwise, immediately reduce your approval rating to −5.

It's now time for a political score check. If your approval rating is worse than −5, turn to p. 149. Otherwise turn to p. 153.

YOUR APPROVAL RATING IS WORSE THAN −5

You've reached Parliament's summer recess and are glad to get a break. The conflict in the Middle East has settled to a tentative truce and energy prices are in retreat. The warmer weather also means there's less need for people to turn on the heating, so it feels like the country has passed the worst of the cost-of-living crisis. It's been a bruising time for you as chancellor, undoubtedly, but brighter days beckon.

But your mood darkens during your much-needed summer vacation when you see the following front-page news story in *The Times*, causing you to sit up in your sunlounger and set down your pina colada.

PM CONSIDERS SACKING CHANCELLOR IN SHOCK PRE-ELECTION RESHUFFLE

The prime minister is considering firing her chancellor in a shock reshuffle ahead of the next general election, as patience in No. 10 wears thin over the performance of Britain's finance minister.

The reshuffle, which is expected as soon as Parliament returns from its summer holiday, is seen as necessary by the prime minister to refresh her top team and cull underperformers before the crunch national vote later this year, according to Downing Street sources.

cont. on p.150

> The chancellor's position is particularly in doubt because of a recent string of decisions that have angered the public.
>
> 'The chancellor has become a deadweight around the neck of this government,' said one ally of the prime minister. 'It can't go on much longer.'

Your reading is interrupted by a spookily timed incoming call from the prime minister herself. You feel a quiver of fear as you pick up the phone.

'You haven't seen it, have you?' she asks.

You say you're looking at it right now.

'Oh. Sorry. I was hoping to speak to you first. Anyway, not to worry. The story is *total and utter nonsense.* I'm baffled. Classic political journalism. They just print any old thing to fill the paper. I'm calling the editor to complain.'

You accept the PM's reassurances with grace but have a strong feeling of unease when you hang up. That unease only deepens when you return to Westminster in September and your schedule of engagement with the prime minister disappears. Given you have a Budget to plan, an election strategy to coordinate, a party conference speech to prepare, you'd have thought Emily might want to meet frequently to discuss such things. But instead her diary is mysteriously chock-a-block, filled with private meetings. And even when you do bump into her – in the evenings, or as you're passing through 10 Downing Street – you sense a coldness and a detachment that is unnerving.

Matters come to a head after the first Prime Minister's Questions (PMQs) session of the new parliamentary term, the weekly session where the PM fields questions from MPs for half an hour in the House of Commons. Polly had been in a panic all morning because there'd been fresh rumours of an imminent Cabinet reshuffle, and the fact you'd still heard of no such thing from the prime minister was foreboding. A reorganisation of the government planned without your input could only mean one thing. Your worst fears are confirmed at the end of PMQs when you get a tap on the shoulder from one of the PM's parliamentary aides, who whispers that the prime minister would like to see you immediately in her office.

This is when you know the game is up. The prime minister's parliamentary office, just behind the Speaker's Chair in the Commons, is famously the place where sackings are conducted on a reshuffle day, to spare the minister the embarrassment of walking up to 10 Downing Street in plain view of the world's media just before they get fired. You enter feeling trepidation.

'I'm sure you know what I'm about to say,' the prime minister says. For a moment you consider saying that no, no you don't, given her denial of the newspaper article, but it feels churlish, so you remain silent.

'Thank you for everything you've done,' she continues. 'But I can't ignore the polls. No hard feelings. I hope I can still count on your support on the backbenches. And I hope we can still be friends.'

You're glassy-eyed as you duck into your ministerial car for the short drive back to the Treasury afterwards, perhaps the last time you'll ever have use of the vehicle. Polly is tearful when you share the news; June offers a consoling hand on the shoulder. Your mind is already racing with the sadness of the moments ahead: of having to say goodbye to all your officials and aides; of having to pack up the No. 11 flat; of seeing your despondent face on the next day's front pages, the highest-profile recipient of a P45 from the PM; the political obituaries they'll write about you, poring over where it went wrong. Another sobering thought hits you: never again will you hold such power. Your ministerial career has reached its climax and now it's back to political obscurity.

Commiserations! Your time as chancellor has come to an end. Return to p. 126 to try again!

PART 3

The Final Stretch

*The Budget is a privilege for the chancellor
because it turns you briefly into the most
powerful person in the government.*

Jeremy Hunt

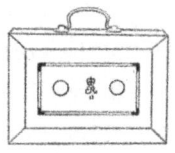

CHAPTER 16

Let the Budget Countdown Begin

*You've got to represent the voice of discipline
when all around you will be undisciplined.*
Philip Hammond

You return from the summer break and Westminster is abuzz with the fresh feeling of a new school term: MPs in shiny new suits, Parliament Square drenched in September sun, your officials and aides sporting healthy tans and reinvigorated for the trials ahead. Your party conference speech, a trip to the International Monetary Fund (IMF), the Budget, a general election … It's going to be a seismic few months.

You meet the prime minister in the garden of 10 Downing Street to discuss big-picture strategy. She's buzzing with ideas about how to win the election, starting with your conference speech and then the Budget.

'We've got to keep slapping voters round the face with goodies,' she says. 'So how about this. Party conference. We bring back the triple lock. Huge giveaway for pensioners who always turn up on polling day. Shore up the grey vote.

Then the Budget. We cut income tax. Pounds in everyone's pockets.'

Your smile at the PM's enthusiasm masks an internal worry about the costs of what she's proposing. You can almost picture Sir Alex's raised eyebrows. The triple lock – which is a guarantee to increase the state pension by the rate of inflation, wage growth or 2.5 per cent, whichever is highest – is a famously expensive commitment that your predecessor had dropped to save money. And cutting income tax is also notoriously costly.

You say you'll do your best but can't make any promises because it all depends on the public finances. Emily puts a hand on your shoulder with a grip that is ever-so-slightly firmer than you might expect and says: 'Chancellor, I know we'll get this right. Especially on income tax. We need that big, simple offer which the public will remember at the ballot box. I have faith in you.'

Sir Alex is predictably alarmed when you inform him of the prime minister's requests, though he promises to present you with full costings of the policies as necessary.

'I'm not saying it's impossible,' he says. 'Far from it. It just might require some … prioritisation.'

You're in two minds about the triple lock move as your party conference speech approaches, on the one hand egged on by Polly who shares the prime minister's view of its electoral value, and on the other dissuaded by June who thinks it's a giveaway too far. With inflation as high as it has been, she points out, it'll be particularly burdensome to fund.

Matters are complicated, however, when the following article appears in the *Daily Express*:

Chancellor Considers Reinstating Triple Lock in Pre-Election Pensioner Boost

The Chancellor of the Exchequer is set to hand pensioners an early Christmas present by bringing back the triple lock, with an announcement expected at party conference.

The government is drawing up the plan with half an eye on the general election and to secure a much-needed poll bump, according to Whitehall sources.

'The prime minister is really pushing for this,' one source said. 'And the chancellor gets it too.'

June spends the next few days darkly muttering that she thinks Polly was the source for the story, which Polly vehemently denies and blames on No. 10. But in any event, expectations are elevated as conference nears. The *Express* runs daily front pages as part of a 'Bring Back the Lock' campaign, telling emotive stories of pensioners who've been struggling since the guarantee was removed. You're reading one of these when Sir Alex places the costing analysis on your desk: £6 billion to enact the policy.

'The choice is yours, chancellor,' he says.

It's time to make your next decision.

DECISION

Reinstate the triple lock. You agree with Polly and the prime minister. Pensioners reliably turn out to vote, so who better to win over with a big announcement like this. You also believe in protecting the elderly and being generous with those who are vulnerable and who've paid taxes all their lives. *Deduct £6 billion from your surplus.* If you choose this option, turn to p. 160.

If you choose this option, turn to p. 160.

OFFICIAL – SENSITIVE

DECISION

Make no change. You agree with June. Of course you'd like to help pensioners, but the cost of the triple lock is too steep, especially with the recent high levels of inflation. You want to keep a sensible grip on the public finances, particularly with the Budget looming. No cost. If you choose this option, turn to p. 162.

OFFICIAL – SENSITIVE

YOU REINSTATE THE TRIPLE LOCK

The jamboree of party conference season – when the nation's politicians decamp to places like Liverpool, Manchester, Birmingham or Brighton to press the flesh with their party faithful and wile away the early hours at corporate-sponsored cocktail parties and cheesy karaoke nights – has never been one of your favourite times in the political calendar. It's even less so now given that you've got a Budget to prepare and an election to win. But you stoically get through this one regardless, Polly plying you with medication to stave off the dreaded conference flu and your nerves building ahead of your big keynote speech. Despite her diminutive stature, June does a fine job shielding you from enterprising reporters as you make your way through the conference hall when the moment arrives, the media peppering you with questions about whether you're bringing back the triple lock.

'If you'd just let the chancellor pass, then you'll soon find out,' June says, swiping away a fluffy-headed microphone that had been thrust in your path.

You're introduced to the stage with a slick video of you in action accompanied by an upbeat pop song selected by Polly, and you feel like a rockstar amid the cheers and applause as you approach the podium. There's a special atmosphere at a pre-election conference like this, the gathered masses expectant and eager for the battle ahead. Whatever the public might think of you outside these four walls, these are your people and this is home turf. These are your door-knockers, leaflet-distributors, local councillors, canvassers, the ground infantry of the coming campaign. And in their minds, you're their second-most senior commander.

There's a trusty formula for a well-received conference speech: recount the biggest achievements of your government, make some pointed jokes about the opposition, lean heavily on your party's favourite slogans. Your version of this is met by rolling waves of increasingly rapturous applause and you build to your final flourish. 'Yes,' you say, 'we are indeed bringing back the triple lock,' prompting a standing ovation as you leave the stage.

'Impeccable work, chancellor,' Polly says, raising you a glass of tap water, grimacing through her conference hangover. 'But maybe next time don't get them to clap so much. Spare a thought for the fragile.'

Your triple lock announcement gets an approving write-up across the papers and none more so than in the *Express*, which claims victory for its campaign.

'*The chancellor and prime minister have listened to the concerns of ordinary, hard-working, upstanding citizens and are to be applauded,*' their leader column declares. '*Pensioners deserve every protection from the government, and may the triple lock never be in doubt again.*'

Add two points to your approval rating.

It's now time to check your economic score.
If your surplus is negative, turn to p. 165.
Otherwise turn to p. 167.

YOU MAKE NO CHANGE

The annual party conference season – when Westminster goes on recess and the nation's politicos descend on cities such as Liverpool, Manchester, Brighton or Birmingham to convene with their party faithful and drink warm white wine at overcrowded drinks receptions – has never been one of your favourite times in the political calendar. It's even less so this year with a Budget to prepare and an election to plan. What's more, you're dreading your conference speech: expectations are in the wrong place on the triple lock, and you fear that your disappointment for pensioners will overshadow everything.

'Support our campaign to bring back the triple lock!' one plucky party volunteer says to you as you make your way through the conference centre, offering you a pamphlet, before it dawns on them too late who you are. June accepts the flier on your behalf and deposits it in the next bin.

You try to keep a low profile throughout proceedings and make it through to your speech without picking up the dreaded conference flu, Polly's plentiful supplies of medication a saving grace. Thunderous applause greets you when it's your turn on stage, your opening backdrop a flashy promo video showing you in action: here in a hard hat at a building site, then surrounded by construction workers, then pointing at machinery, and all to the soundtrack of an upbeat pop walkout song selected by Polly. As you wave to the gathered masses and approach the podium you figure this is the closest you'll ever get to a rockstar reception. These are your people, this is a home fixture. You can also see how much this means to them. An election is looming and this is your ground army, your collection of canvassers, councillors, door-knockers and leafleters who will be crucial to securing another five years in power. And like any good army, they need good commanders, and you're the most senior one they have after the prime minister.

As you're reflecting on your speech afterwards, you figure that 95 per cent of it was a success. The tried-and-tested recipe of listing your government's greatest achievements, making fun of your political opponents and liberally referencing the party's favourite political slogans had delivered wave after wave of enthusiastic clapping and cheers. But the final 5 per cent was quite awful. You could feel the expectation in the room as you crescendoed to your finale, and then all that good feeling dissipating with your sober declaration that no, alas, the triple lock is unaffordable at this time, though of course the government would continue to assess its options. There'd even been a smattering of boos at that point, and that was the clip that led all the evening news broadcasts.

'Just when I thought my life couldn't get any worse,' Polly says as she holds her forehead and clutches a glass of tap water, sitting with you in your hotel room as you watch that evening's BBC 10 o'clock news. Polly had spent all day nursing a hangover from her conference partying excesses, and her mood is sulphurous.

'What is it with the media?' she says. 'An hour of adoration for you from the audience and then ten seconds of booing, and the boos are the headline? Think I might cancel our sit-down with the economics editor.'

You stand Polly down from her retributive plans but share her gloominess. The front pages of the next day's papers are little better, and the *Express* is particularly damning.

'*What an insult it was to Britain's pensioners, after their years of service and contribution to this country, for the chancellor to stand up yesterday and to say we cannot afford their care,*' its leader column declares. '*The triple lock is the very least they deserve, and the chancellor's position is shameful.*'

June is less downbeat, however, when you're taking stock back at the Treasury on your return to London.

'No-one thanks you when you do it, chancellor,' she says. 'But it's so important to say no. I'm proud of you. And there are lots of people in this building who are also very grateful for your discipline.'

Deduct two points from your approval rating.
Now turn to p. 167.

YOUR ECONOMIC SCORE TURNS NEGATIVE AFTER COMMITTING TO THE TRIPLE LOCK

You're still enjoying the warm glow of approving press coverage from the triple lock decision when there's a knock at your door in the study of No. 11 Downing Street and June enters. She's carrying a hefty file and seems displeased.

'We've got away with it for now,' she says. 'But the City has cottoned on. Look.'

June opens her file. It contains various research notes from banks and economists all coming to the same conclusion: that your commitment to the triple lock puts the government on course to breach its fiscal rules. Everyone's put their own estimates on how expensive the policy is, but they've each calculated that it will push you into the red. June reads the following excerpt from a note by JP Morgan:

> The chancellor's significant giveaway to pensioners indicates a near-term risk for UK economic policy: that the government's desire to be re-elected and curry favour with voters risks an abandonment of fiscal prudence and probity. We will have to wait and see the OBR's official verdict at the Budget this autumn. But unless the chancellor is able to find money elsewhere at that set-piece – either through spending cuts or tax increases, which will surely be a difficult sell in

an election year – we calculate the government is on course to miss its fiscal rules.

'I just wanted to flag these as a warning, chancellor,' June says. 'Markets are stable. But we're very much on notice.'

You thank June for her advice and assure her you've got everything under control.

Now turn to p. 167.

CHAPTER 17

The Scorecard

The scorecard runs your life through the whole Budget.
Philip Hammond

The life of the chancellor can often feel like an endless carousel of meetings – with CEOs, MPs, civil servants, aides, the central bank, the OBR, government ministers, businesses, and so on – but you're particularly looking forward to the one at which you arrive the next Monday morning. Its importance is evident in its location and attendees: your private office in the Treasury with Sir Alex chairing proceedings, surrounded by all of the senior directors of the department and their most talented officials, with standing room only for Polly and June. It's the biggest planning meeting yet for the Budget.

'Chancellor, I hope you'll be pleased with what we've prepared,' Sir Alex begins, presenting beside a screen. 'We've been careful to consider the political context in drawing up these ideas.'

Sir Alex explains what the next few weeks will look like. You will go through a process of whittling down options from a menu prepared by the Treasury's brightest and best. The choices will be noted in what's called the 'scorecard' –

effectively a computer spreadsheet which tracks the different decisions that collectively make up the Budget. The official in charge of manning the spreadsheet raises their hand in acknowledgement when introduced by Sir Alex.

'Perhaps the most important person in the British government for the next few weeks,' Sir Alex says with a chuckle. 'Let's just hope he doesn't delete the file or anything.'

Before showing you the menu of options, Sir Alex has a preamble. He urges you not to be daunted by the array of choices. 'We'll work through each of these areas one by one,' he says. He also says it's useful to see all the options in one place at the start of the process so that you can grasp the big picture of what's possible and begin to think about how we can make the numbers add up.

'Without further ado,' he says. 'Voila.'

Policy Area	Options	Cost / Revenue (£ billion)
Public Spending	Cut by 1%	+10
	Hold steady	0
	Increase by 1%	−10
Inheritance Tax	Increase inheritance tax	+4
	No change	0
	Abolish inheritance tax	−7
Fuel Duty	Freeze fuel duty	−5
	Let fuel duty rise	0
Wealth Tax	5% levy on wealth over £5 million, collected over ten years	+5
	No change	0
Sin Taxes	Increase duties on alcohol, tobacco, sugary drinks, flying and vaping	+3
	No change	0
	Cut duties on alcohol, tobacco, sugary drinks, flying and vaping	−3
Welfare	Increase Universal Credit by £20 weekly	−4
	No change	0
	Cut Universal Credit by £20 weekly	+4
National Insurance	Increase National Insurance for businesses	+10
	No change	0
Income Tax	Cut the basic rate by 1%	−7.5
	No change	0

Polly whistles. June squints and slowly nods. You sense she'll enjoy the intellectual challenge of getting this right.

'As I said,' Sir Alex says. 'We're still in the early stages and we don't have to make any decisions today. But it's perhaps helpful to have sight of what's in our armoury.'

You thank Sir Alex and the team for all their preparatory work, and say you look forward to the coming weeks.

'This is where the fun begins,' Sir Alex says.

On p. 341 you'll find a blank scorecard you can use to build your Budget. You can add your choices as you proceed through the coming chapters.

Note: your current budget surplus or deficit is still subject to change before the big day, depending on the forecasts you receive from the OBR. Now turn to p. 171.

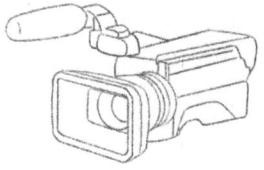

CHAPTER 18

Managing the Media

*There's a lot of pre-Budget pitch-rolling,
leaking things in the media … It's a game.*
Philip Hammond

Polly pulls you aside when the meeting breaks up, says she has something important to discuss. You wait for the final officials to leave and then she begins, elbows on your desk and fingers steepled, her expression cunning.

'I've been thinking about how we handle our dear friends in the media throughout all this,' she says, eyes flicking to Sir Alex's menu. 'I've been doing my research and communications ahead of a Budget is a delicate thing. If we get it wrong and expectations end up in the wrong place, we'll be setting ourselves up for failure. But if we get it right, it can be transformative. Luckily, I am now learned in the dark arts in such matters. Just give me your blessing, chancellor, and the fourth estate will be dancing to our tune.'

You ask Polly if she might give you a hint of what she has in mind. She explains her strategy as follows: yes, we want to save some nice big surprises for the day – the rabbits to be pulled from the magician's hat, so to speak – but we also need to keep the media on side with a steady drip feed of scoops and exclusives in the build-up to Budget Day. 'This has various advantages,' she says. 'First, it will keep the beast of British political journalism happy and stop them from filling the papers with critical coverage and vindictive pieces which would otherwise appear if they felt like we were shutting them out. Second, it will let us draw attention to policies that put us in a good light which would otherwise get lost in the deluge of Budget Day. And third, it builds public interest and awareness in the Budget, which is all good for your own name recognition and profile.'

'I'll also do the classic of telling everyone the cupboards are bare,' she says. 'And then we can try to surprise on the upside.'

You say that perhaps the cupboards are indeed pretty bare.

'Then all the more reason to tell everyone,' Polly says. 'I know the Budget's meant to be this big secret and the Speaker hates it when stuff leaks in the media first. But we need to be shrewd and strategic. It's all about expectations management and that's my forte. Leave the media to me.'

CHAPTER 19

The Public Purse

Some of the public spending things are
excruciatingly difficult. They're hard choices.
Norman Lamont

There's a fresh intensity in the corridors of the Treasury in the ensuing days, the pressure ratcheting higher and higher as the big decisions loom. You're joined in your office by Polly, June, Sir Alex and a clutch of top officials to discuss perhaps the biggest of them all: the level at which to set public spending, a choice that will define the entire Budget.

'It's really up to you how you'd like to handle this, chancellor,' Sir Alex says. 'There's much to be said for each of the various options we propose.'

Polly initially argues for an increase in public spending, saying that putting more money into schools and hospitals would be appealing to voters who value education and the NHS, but her conviction wavers when Sir Alex points out the £10 billion price tag. 'It's certainly an option,' Sir Alex says, 'but it would constrain our choices elsewhere.' June is supportive of a public spending increase – 'It's our duty to provide high-quality public services,' she says – 'but only if it's affordable.'

And Polly is initially opposed to a public spending cut – she fears you'll be accused of that dreaded word, 'austerity' – but her attitude changes when Sir Alex explains a trick used by your predecessors. 'Given an imminent election,' Sir Alex says, 'chancellors have been known to pencil in unrealistically meagre sums for public spending in years beyond the election date, and to use the savings from such meagre assumptions to fund immediate tax cuts.' You can almost see the lightbulb illuminate above Polly's head.

'So that could free up the money to announce an income tax cut just before the election?' she asks eagerly.

Sir Alex removes his glasses, cleans them with a cloth, then replaces them before answering.

'It's not for me to suggest the political merits or otherwise of a potential course of action,' he says. 'But yes, that would indeed be possible. Whether it is an honourable or upstanding way to manage the public finances, I leave for you to decide.'

Polly's expression suggests questions of honour and upstandingness are quite far from her mind. June is frowning, however. She says funding a tax cut in that way may not be seen as credible by the markets and that it will store up problems for whoever is chancellor after the election, because that person will have to address the tight spending plans.

'The future chancellor is sitting right with us,' Polly says, gesturing to you. 'And the point you raise is a problem for another day.'

You thank everyone for their input and turn to the official manning the scorecard. It's time to make your next decision.

Remember, keep the big picture in mind. You can remind yourself of Sir Alex's menu of Budget options for raising taxes and spending revenue on p. 169.

DECISION

Increase public spending by 1 per cent.
You recognise it's the expensive option, but
you want to give a boost to Britain's public
services. You think it's important that areas
such as education and the health service get
the funding they need, and you hope voters will
agree. *Record the decision in your Budget scorecard,
noting the £10 billion cost.* Now turn to p. 176.

No change. You want to keep public spending at
its existing level. *Record the decision in your Budget
scorecard, noting no impact to the public finances.*
Now turn to p. 180.

Cut public spending by 1 per cent. You expect
it may be unpopular in some parts, but you
want to free up cash for other priorities. You're
attracted by Polly's argument and think you can
use a public spending cut to your advantage.
*Record the decision in your Budget scorecard, noting
the £10 billion gain.* Now turn to p. 178.

OFFICIAL – SENSITIVE

YOU DECIDE TO INCREASE
PUBLIC SPENDING BY 1 PER CENT

Your decision draws cautious nods of approval from the Treasury officials around the table.

'Very good, chancellor,' Sir Alex says. 'The parameters have been set.'

Polly joins you in the No. 11 study later that evening to explain her plan for how to spin the uplift to the media. She thinks this is one of those good news stories that's worth getting out there ahead of Budget Day so the public have time to digest your generosity.

'I'll tell the papers times are tight but we're looking at a £5 billion increase for schools and hospitals,' she says. 'We don't want to be too dour about things. Let the public know we care. And then bam! £10 billion on Budget Day. Pitch-rolling par excellence.'

To Polly's credit, her planting of seeds about your public spending intentions succeeds. Britain's chief political commentators broadly welcome the idea that you're set to put more money into the NHS and education, calling it the approach of a responsible chancellor who's looking beyond the immediate pressures of the election.

'*Chancellors have been known to play fast and loose with the public finances before a national vote to deliver a sugar rush for voters,*' one such commentator writes. '*It's admirable if this chancellor is resisting that temptation. There are few better things the government can be spending money on than the health of the nation and the education of our children, so the chancellor has our full backing if that's the intention.'*

Your spending plans are asked about in various focus groups and a reassuring verdict returns: the public is supportive and they view you more positively as a result.

Add one point to your approval rating.
Now turn to p. 181.

YOU CUT PUBLIC SPENDING BY 1 PER CENT

Polly congratulates you when the meeting is over, says you've freed up firepower to use ahead of the election. She also sets out her plan for how to spin the story to the media.

'We have to over-egg it,' she says. 'Tell the press there's a big hole in the public finances that needs filling. A shortfall of £20 billion, something like that. And then boom! We deliver only a £10 billion cut to public spending on Budget Day. We turn bad news into good news.'

Polly sets about planting her seeds of pessimism with journalists in the coming days, and if anything her expectation-setting is a little bit too effective. 'Chancellor Faces Bombshell Budget Black Hole,' writes the *Sun*. 'Hair-Shirt Budget in Store,' reports the *Guardian*. 'Bad Old Days of Austerity Loom,' says the *Daily Mirror*.

'*Rumours that the chancellor is preparing swingeing cuts to public spending are very troubling indeed,*' the *Mirror*'s leader column notes. '*One can only hope that this is not a creative accounting exercise in the Treasury to gin up funds for transient pre-election tax cuts. Strong, well-funded public services are the bedrock of social stability, and the chancellor shouldn't forget that.*'

You start to feel a little worried as the national conversation continues to focus on your impending Budget cutbacks in the following days and your poll ratings take a hit, but Polly says everything is going to plan.

'Let them tell their horror stories,' she says. 'It'll make our £10 billion cut look even more generous on the day.'

Deduct one point from your approval rating.
Now turn to p. 181.

YOU MAKE NO CHANGE
TO PUBLIC SPENDING

Your decision is duly entered into the scorecard and Sir Alex straightens his glasses.

'Very good, chancellor,' he says. 'A balanced approach.'

Polly lingers when the meeting is over and tells you she has a plan for how to spin this decision to your advantage.

'It's all about framing,' she says. 'If we make everyone think that spending cuts are coming, they'll be praising your generosity on Budget Day when they don't materialise.'

Polly's hint-dropping and rumour-spreading with various trusted journalists begins to bear fruit in the coming days, the press writing pieces about a panicking Treasury and spooked chancellor preparing to unveil the bitter medicine of spending cutbacks. Polly instructs the Treasury press office to pointedly not deny such reports and asks you to do your very best to seem downbeat and frustrated when appearing in public, giving the media the perfect photos to illustrate their pessimistic reports.

'Oscar-worthy stuff, chancellor,' Polly says, holding up a latest press picture of you with furrowed brow entering the Treasury at the end of the week. 'At this rate, flat public spending will seem like manna from heaven.'

Now turn to p. 181.

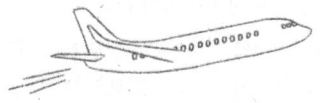

CHAPTER 20

To Stay or to Go?

There's a lot of value in building relationships with
your foreign counterparts so that, when you do come
to a crisis, you know the people you're dealing with.
Philip Hammond

While your busy Budget work continues, your autumn schedule also includes regular chancellor engagements and next up is a trip to Washington, DC for the annual meetings of the IMF and World Bank. These are important get-togethers with finance ministers from across the globe where you discuss shared challenges and collaborate on potential solutions. Economic sanctions against rogue states, emergency loans to struggling nations, bilateral chats that might unlock future trade deals … these are the weighty conversations that happen behind closed doors and it's your job to advocate for the United Kingdom. It's also a chance to build relationships with fellow powerbrokers that could be crucial in future crises. Preparations for the trip are complicated, however, by a breaking scandal in Westminster.

'Have you seen the *Guardian*?' Polly asks, breathlessly entering your office the day before you're due to fly. 'The timing couldn't be worse.'

She shows you the article. Through freedom of information requests and diligent number crunching, the paper has revealed a staggering abuse of overseas travel and expenses by MPs and government ministers in recent years, all funded by the taxpayer. The list makes painful reading: hundreds of thousands of pounds spent on umpteen spurious trips to the Seychelles by junior ministers in the transport department; the finest champagne and caviar enjoyed by numerous members of a parliamentary committee while flying business class to various 'fact-finding' missions in exotic locations; luxury accommodation and Michelin star dining in Vietnam for Foreign Office special advisors; the environment secretary (!) using a private jet to fly within the UK for visits and to get to other European capitals easily reachable by train; the deputy prime minister spending more time on tours of sub-Saharan Africa, Central America and India than being in Britain over the last year.

'We are being taken for fools,' the *Guardian*'s leader column booms. 'As night follows day, politicians just can't help themselves. We send them to Westminster to act on our behalf, but inevitably they act for themselves. This newspaper thought that the political class would've learnt their lesson from the last expenses scandal that destroyed trust in British politics. How wrong we were.'

You tell Polly that this is obviously regrettable, but you don't see the immediate problem.

'Keep reading,' she says.

'And perhaps most galling of all,' the column continues, 'is the conduct of the Treasury. The government department we entrust with our hard-earned money has been the worst offender in all of this. The travel log and expense filings of the former chancellor are frankly staggering. The frequent trips to Dubai, the flashy hotels, the special advisors indulging in every extravagance on the public *purse ... while we recognise there has been a change of personnel at the top of the Treasury, this is nevertheless a day of shame for our finance ministry.'*

'Now you see the problem,' she says.

You huddle with your advisors and debate what to do. Polly says you obviously have to cancel the IMF trip. She says she's the first person to enjoy a good jolly, but it would look tin-eared to go abroad now. She says cancellation would send an appropriate message of restraint and apology for the excesses of the past, even if they weren't directly your doing.

'The press will have a field day otherwise,' she says. 'I've already had journalists get in touch asking if it's going ahead.'

But June disagrees. She says these international gatherings are a vital part of your role, and you shouldn't let a bit of domestic drama distract you. Especially when you personally haven't done anything wrong. Polly's suggestion that you just join the meetings by video conference is met with a June eyeroll.

'The value comes from being there face to face,' June says. 'The informal exchanges you have on the sidelines. The dinners and drinks with your counterparts where the real business is done. We'd miss all that.'

You thank them for their counsel and call in your private secretary who'd arranged the logistics of the IMF visit. It's time to make your next decision.

DECISION

Go ahead with the trip. You agree with June. You want to do your best to represent the UK on the world stage and advocate for Britain's interests. You recognise you may get some criticism for going given the mood in Westminster, but your work as chancellor is more important. If you choose this option, turn to p. 186.

OFFICIAL – SENSITIVE

DECISION

Cancel the trip. You agree with Polly. You're worried about the potential media backlash from going, especially with an election drawing closer and closer. Cancelling will show that you're in tune with public opinion and focused on domestic priorities. There's a time and place for a trip like this, and now is neither. If you choose this option, turn to p. 189.

OFFICIAL – SENSITIVE

YOU GO AHEAD WITH THE TRIP

Your time at the IMF is a flurry of photo ops, handshakes and speed-reading briefing notes between meetings – brushing up on the latest trade talks with Canada, reminding yourself of the UK's sanctions stance versus Iran, picking out some recently announced steel tariffs you wanted to discreetly raise with the US Treasury secretary – and on that count the visit is a diplomatic success. You've extracted concessions on each of these issues and proudly stand in the family photo at the end of proceedings, lined up with your fellow finance ministers, congratulating yourself on a job well done. Polly has been trying to get your attention throughout, however, but you've been too busy and it's only before your final media huddle with a select group of travelling journalists that you have a chance to catch up.

'I know you want to talk about trade, and sanctions, and progress on tariffs,' Polly says. 'But all they're going to ask you about is why you've come. The papers have been going potty back home.'

Sure enough, you spend the entirety of your interrogation by the media defending your presence in Washington, the gathered reporters unimpressed by your claim to have made significant progress on matters of international economic policy important to the UK. June is at your side during the briefing and eventually snaps.

'Doesn't anyone have a question about a matter of substance?' she interrupts, eyeballing the press pack. 'On the things that actually matter?'

This only draws more sceptical looks and frowned scribbles. You finally have a chance to assess the damage on the flight home – you're in economy, despite June's protestations that the chancellor obviously deserves better – as you flick through the media cuttings prepared by Polly. The opinion column by the *Guardian*'s chief political commentator sums it up.

Jet-set Chancellor Rubs Salt in the Wound after Travel Expenses Scandal

At a time when the public might have expected some prudence and humility from the government on the question of jet-setting at the taxpayer's expense – particularly from the Treasury – we're treated to the spectacle of our chancellor swaggering across the Atlantic to chin-wag and shmooze with the global financial elite for no apparent gain whatsoever. So much hot air is produced at these IMF gatherings that the chancellor could've inflated a balloon with it all and flown back for free. But no. Once again, we're picking up the tab.

'The next time the *Guardian* wants an exclusive from us, I'll tell them where to go,' Polly mutters darkly.

Your perusal of the rest of the papers reveals a similar verdict and it's only buried deep in the inner pages of the financial and business press that you find any mention of your wins from the meetings. The effect of all this negative media coverage begins to show in the latest opinion polls, and your reputation takes a hit.

Matters get even worse in the following days when you get a crucial pre-Budget update from the OBR. It's their job to give you a series of forecasts in the run-up to the big day, and their predictions for economic growth can have a big impact on your surplus and how much breathing space you have to meet your fiscal rules. The latest numbers from the OBR aren't good: they're now predicting weaker economic growth than previously forecast, an overhang of the higher interest rates from the Bank and the impact of the energy crisis earlier in the year.

'The blimmin' OBR,' June says through gritted teeth, reviewing the numbers with you. 'It's not easy this chancellor lark, is it?'

Deduct two points from your approval rating and £2 billion from your surplus. Now turn to p. 191.

YOU STAY AT HOME

Cancel the travel, you tell your private secretary, much to Polly's pleasure.

'I'll tell the press straight away,' Polly says.

The *Guardian*'s chief political commentator is the first to congratulate you online when the news breaks, claiming your decision as a victory for the paper's journalism and a win for the taxpayer. You're expecting the rest of the British media to follow suit, but instead something strange happens. A counter-argument swells, initiated by the *Daily Mail*.

'*Isn't the chancellor supposed to be out there batting for Britain?*' asks their most famous columnist, replying to the *Guardian*'s comment. '*Do we really want global economic affairs to be run by everyone else? Have we given up our seat at the table so easily? MPs taking the mickey with expenses is one thing, but the chancellor representing us on the world stage is something else.*'

The baton is picked up by others in the right-leaning press, the *Daily Express* and the *Sun* also expressing alarm that you're skipping the meetings in Washington. 'Britain's AWOL Chancellor' is the verdict of the former. 'IMF? More Like WFH!' says the latter.

You're surveying the papers in your Treasury office when you're joined by Sir Alex. He gives you a knowing look.

'I've seen this happen before,' he says, sliding his spectacles down the bridge of his nose. 'There's a real jealousy between the papers. No doubt they wish they'd done the *Guardian*'s investigation. And this is their chance to marginalise it. To hit back. To say it doesn't really matter. Unfortunately, that means attacking you.'

Polly's disbelief deepens when the opposition jumps on the bandwagon and tables an Urgent Question in Parliament demanding to know why you've skipped the IMF meetings. Normally your political opponents complain if you don't turn up to answer a Urgent Question in the Commons, but this time it's the opposite. 'Why are you here, chancellor?' they cry, as you stand to defend yourself at the despatch box. 'Get on a plane, chancellor!'

Then you learn of another setback as you're leaving Parliament. June is with you in your ministerial car as it snakes back to the Treasury, and she says the OBR's latest pre-Budget forecasts are in. These numbers are vital because the OBR's predictions for economic growth affect your surplus and how much breathing space you have in meeting your fiscal rules. She says the numbers aren't good: the OBR is forecasting weaker growth than previously expected, a consequence of the fallout from the recent energy crisis and elevated interest rates.

'Oh, the OBR,' she sighs. 'When will they give us a break?'

Deduct one point from your approval rating and £2 billion from your surplus. Now turn to p. 191.

CHAPTER 21

Never Enough

It's a bit like a game of bridge.
Both sides are trying to bluff the other.
Norman Lamont on running a Spending Review

With the IMF shenanigans behind you, you finally get a chance to knuckle down in your Treasury office for a few days on Budget preparations. However, just as you're reviewing the official advice on whether to tweak inheritance tax, you hear sudden shouting and a door slam from the adjacent room. There is a scurrying of footsteps in the corridor and further commotion. Polly looks at you with alarm.

'Spending Review going well then,' she says. 'That didn't sound like a balloon pop.'

You go to investigate and find your deputy – the Chief Secretary to the Treasury, Simon Miser – pale-faced and slumped in his chair next door. The balloon remnants at his feet are the signs of the successes of recent days, popped in traditional celebration whenever a government department agrees to its spending allocation for the coming years, a famously tense negotiating process known as the Spending Review that's overseen by the chief secretary and due to be announced alongside your Budget. You'd set the overall level of public spending and Simon had been divvying up that pot between the different ministries. Yet two balloons remain conspicuously floating behind him. They're labelled 'Health' and 'Defence'.

'We have a problem, chancellor,' Simon says. 'They're both holding out for more. Much more.'

Simon is about to explain further but Sir Alex interrupts. He says the health secretary and defence secretary want to speak to you urgently. Apparently, they'd made a beeline for your office after meeting the chief secretary but your enterprising diary manager had intercepted them and is appeasing them with tea and biscuits down the hall.

'May I suggest, chancellor,' Sir Alex says, 'that you steel yourself for this encounter.'

You take stock with Polly, June and Simon in your office – reacquainting yourself with the latest budgets for the NHS and MOD, rehearsing your justification for your decision on the level of public spending – and call them in.

First to enter is the health secretary, Harry Spital. One of the highest-profile members of the Cabinet, Harry is known to harbour intense leadership ambitions and is one of the best communicators and networkers in Westminster. Whenever the conversation turns to future prime ministers, his name inevitably comes up. You've always had a good relationship with Harry, but you also sense a low-level enmity towards you because of your higher-ranking position as chancellor. His causing a fuss here is no surprise: being seen to stand up for the NHS is good for his personal brand and you predict he'll milk this for all it's worth.

'Chancellor,' he says, passing a hand through slicked-back hair. 'No doubt you know why we're here.'

Behind him emerges the defence secretary, Milly Terry. Her presence is more surprising. One of the older members of your political party, Milly had an illustrious career in the forces before entering politics and has a reputation as a staunch loyalist who'd never once rebelled against the government during her 30 years in Parliament. Her leadership ambitions are the opposite of Harry's: non-existent. And that makes her standing here all the more worrying. If she's digging in, it must be a matter of principle.

'It gives us no pleasure to have to do this, chancellor,' Milly says. 'But you've given us no choice.'

'The public spending envelope is beyond inadequate,' Harry says. 'It's insulting.'

Both ministers then give variations of the same speech. For Harry, it's a doomsday account of the massive pressures on the NHS: the aging population, the lengthy waiting lists, the lack of beds, the remorseless winter crises, the long delays in A&E, the staff shortages, the indignity of patients being treated in corridors, the crumbling hospitals. 'The only solution to all of this is more money,' he says. 'Lots of it.'

For Milly, it's a sober intonement on the growing threats facing Britain. The proliferation of nuclear weapons, the rise of cyberwarfare, the burgeoning strength of our adversaries, the increasingly sophisticated methods and weaponry of our foes, all at a time when our own armed forces, navy and Royal Air Force are hollowed out and in desperate need of upgrades. 'For the security of our nation,' she says, 'we simply must be given more.'

You're about to thank them for raising their concerns and respond with some points of your own but Harry isn't finished.

'Chancellor, be in no doubt how serious we consider this,' he says. 'Frankly, it's a resignation matter. For both of us. We couldn't continue in these roles in good conscience otherwise.'

That's an escalation that catches you off-guard. Ministers kicking up a fuss over their departmental budgets during a Spending Review is nothing new – if anything, it's expected and all part of the game – but to threaten to quit is something else. You foresee how damaging the resignations would be – all the headlines about a divided government, the likely attacks you'd face from Harry and Milly's parliamentary supporters, the papers filled with Westminster naval-gazing and psycho-drama, a sure-fire turn-off for the electorate when you can least afford it. Harry's smile suggests he's made these calcula-tions too. As a final flourish, he brandishes an already-written resignation letter bearing both his and Milly's signature.

'We're ready to hand this to the prime minister this evening unless there is movement from the Treasury,' he says. 'We're sure you'll make the right decision. For the health and security of this great nation.'

Polly slates the pair of them when they've gone, but also credits their savviness.

'It's a win–win for them, isn't it?' she says. 'If we fold, they're the heroes who stood up for the NHS and defence of the realm. If we stand firm, they go out in a principled blaze of glory. And it leaves Harry perfectly positioned for a run at the leadership if we lose the election, or alternatively ripe for reappointment to the Cabinet in a post-election reshuffle if we win. It's clever politics.'

June's view is that this is standard Spending Review brinksmanship and that you should obviously reject their request for more money. 'You set public spending at the level you did for good reason,' she reminds you. 'Probity in the public finances must come first,' she says, 'regardless of special pleading from ministers. And who knows? Maybe it's all a bluff and they won't resign.' Simon concurs. 'We have to say no,' he says.

But Polly thinks differently. She views their resignation threat as credible and says it's in your best interests to avoid a big Cabinet bust-up before the election. 'A few extra billion pounds on hospitals and troops is worth it to keep the peace,' she says.

It's time to make your next decision.

DECISION

Accept their demands and give more money to the NHS and defence. You agree with Polly. You want to preserve Cabinet unity and avoid invoking the ire of two senior politicians. The last thing you want is a news cycle about splits and division. It'll mean a further outlay from the public purse, but you deem it worth it. *Deduct £2 billion from your surplus.* Now turn to p. 198.

OFFICIAL – SENSITIVE

DECISION

Reject their demands. You agree with June and Simon. You have every sympathy for the cases made by Harry and Milly, but the money simply isn't there. The resignation threat is a worry, certainly, but it also might not materialise. It's your job to keep a tight grip on public spending, and that means taking a stand here. No cost. Now turn to p. 200.

OFFICIAL – SENSITIVE

YOU ACCEPT THEIR DEMANDS

You invite Harry and Milly to join you in your study in No. 11 Downing Street later that evening for an update on the Spending Review, and you share the good news.

'Absolutely brilliant, chancellor,' Harry says, shaking your hand with gusto. 'The nation's doctors and nurses thank you.'

'As do our brave armed forces,' Milly says. 'This is an act of genuine patriotism.'

The pair have barely left Downing Street when the news is already breaking online, framed as an almighty Treasury capitulation in the face of a brave rearguard action led by the health secretary.

'Spital Extracts Vital NHS Funds from Cautious Chancellor,' says the *Guardian*.

'NHS Saved by Spital's Treasury Showdown,' says the *Daily Mirror*.

'Spital Secures Extra Cash Injection for the NHS,' says the BBC.

'Why is no-one reporting about the extra money for the MOD?' June asks, looking at her phone in puzzlement.

'Because this is all being briefed by Mr Slick Back,' Polly says. 'What an operator. Milly's heart is genuinely in the right place. But Mr H. Spital was playing politics. And he's played it well. Better these headlines than the spectacle of Cabinet in-fighting, though. We had no choice.'

'I still think they were bluffing,' June says. 'I guess we'll never know.'

Now turn to p. 203.

YOU REJECT THEIR DEMANDS

You ask Harry and Milly to come over to 11 Downing Street that evening and you explain your decision, describing it as regrettable but necessary given the state of the public finances. Harry seems genuinely surprised. Milly is stony-faced.

'I thought you were better than this, chancellor,' Harry says. 'This is no time for Treasury orthodoxy and penny-pinching. Last chance. Give us the money or we're going straight to the prime minister.'

You explain that doing so will do them little good. You've discussed your decision with the PM and she's given you her full backing. And your decision is final.

'Then so be it,' Harry says. 'This is your doing, not ours.'

Within minutes of leaving Downing Street their resignation letter is going viral online, Britain's political journalists gripped by the drama of a government bun-fight. The letter reads:

Dear Prime Minister,

It's been the privilege of our lives to serve you in government. Every day we've fought our hardest for the health and security of the United Kingdom. The doctors and nurses in the NHS, alongside our brave servicemen and women, represent truly the best of this great nation and it's been an honour to act on their behalf. There is nothing more important than the wellbeing and security of Britain.

And it is because of this belief that we see no alternative but to resign our posts today. We fear that the Treasury, and particularly the chancellor, have lost sight of the fundamental duties of government and where its priorities should lie. We cannot in good conscience continue to lead our departments when we know they are being starved of the funding they so desperately need. Our chancellor is setting us up for failure.

We are deeply saddened that the chancellor is not committing sufficient resources to the vital areas we represent, and even more so that the Treasury has ignored our reasonable requests for a change of course. Please do not interpret this letter as anything other than a patriotic cry for help from two dedicated public servants who want nothing more than for this country to be safe and prosperous. We fear the same cannot be said of other senior members in your government.

You will, of course, continue to enjoy our fulsome support from the backbenches and vigorous backing in the upcoming election campaign. Should the opportunity to serve arise again in future, we stand ready to seize it.

Kind regards,

H. Spital and Milly Terry

'What rapscallions,' Polly says. 'No bad feelings towards Milly, she genuinely cares. But trust Harry to turn this into a big attack on you. He's always thinking about the leadership.'

The next day's front pages are a clean sweep on the resignation drama and there are many column inches dedicated to the assault on you and the Treasury.

'Knives Out for the Chancellor,' declares the *Sun*.

'Chancellor Excoriated in Cabinet Ambush,' says the *Guardian*.

'Government at War over NHS, Defence Budgets,' says the *Daily Mail*.

The former health secretary even does the morning broadcast round to criticise you further, touring the TV studios with the tale of a helpless NHS ravaged by a heartless Treasury and chancellor, lapping up the limelight.

'I'm not one to advocate violence,' Polly says, as you're listening to Spital's latest broadside against you on LBC Radio. 'But boy does he push me.'

The media frenzy around the story lasts a full week, the news agenda otherwise quiet and the nation's political correspondents happy to eke out a palace intrigue story for everything it's worth. You end up taking such a beating from the commentariat that you debate whether to come out and defend yourself, but Sir Alex persuades you to stand down.

'Wise to stay above the fray, chancellor,' he says. 'We're the ones who have to make the hard choices and make the numbers add up. A dignified silence befits you here.'

Deduct two points from your approval rating.
Now turn to p. 203.

CHAPTER 22

The Death Tax

*The Budget is one of the few parliamentary
occasions when members of the public
take any notice of Westminster.*
Gordon Brown, Chancellor of the Exchequer, 1997–2007

It's an historic feature of British democracy that even the most
senior ministers in the government – including you, the chancellor – continue to represent constituents as a Member of
Parliament, and hence one day you can be speaking with the
Governor of the Bank of England about maintaining stability
in the global economy, and the next you're sat with sweet little
Doreen from down the road who's having trouble getting her
free bus pass. And it's as you're hosting your weekly Friday
constituency surgery – a chance for anyone in your local area
to raise a grievance, be it trouble getting their benefits, the lack
of quality schooling in the area or the road closure causing
misery along their lane – that you're confronted by a woman
who immediately breaks down in tears.

'Chancellor, you have to help me,' she says, struggling to
speak through the sobbing. 'It's appalling what the government is doing to me.'

You listen to her case with concern. She explains that her mother, a widower, recently died from a sudden illness. She has inherited the family home as a result, a treasured property that's been with them for generations, filled with heirlooms and happy memories. Despite only burying her mother a few days ago, she's now facing a £100,000 inheritance tax bill.

'£100,000!' she says. 'It's just so cruel. Of course I don't have £100,000. I'm still grieving Mum and now I've got the worry of the taxman knocking on my door and the only way I can pay is by selling our home. It's horrible.'

You ask her if she's sure that the tax liability is correct and she reveals the sums. They do add up: inheritance tax is charged at 40 per cent on estates above a £325,000 tax-free threshold, with the threshold rising to £500,000 when inheriting a property from a parent. The woman's family home is worth £750,000 so, yes, £100,000 is the tax she must pay.

'Surely there's something you can do, isn't there chancellor?' she pleads. You have to disappoint her: 'Tax policy is set at the Budget,' you say, 'and unfortunately for now the law of the land is as it is.' While you'd like to help, you say, it would be inappropriate for the chancellor to intervene ad hoc in individual tax cases. The woman storms out of your surgery with fresh tears.

Her story troubles you and you recount it to Sir Alex in your Treasury office the following Monday. He says your constituent was certainly unfortunate. He reminds you that inheritance tax can be avoided if assets are transferred from a parent to a beneficiary more than seven years before their death, a get-out clause that people often try to use.

'But alas, the date of one's death is famously unknowable,' he says. 'And not everyone has the wherewithal or foresight to arrange their tax affairs accordingly.'

Your constituent's experience is weighing on your mind as you review your Budget plans for inheritance tax, one of the areas where your officials have proposed reforms. Polly has been in your ear suggesting you scrap the tax entirely, saying it would be a popular move that would end the kind of heartache you'd seen first-hand. You're also aware that it's an idea supported by the prime minister.

However, as your briefing note from your civil servants points out, the tax raises almost £7 billion annually which you can spend on public services. Your officials also note that the tax is targeted more towards the wealthy and is levied on those who need the money least: the deceased. As a mechanism for transferring wealth from the better-off to the needy, they say, the tax has its merits, and hence you may even wish to consider increasing it.

You call June for her view and she's cautious. Her take is that abolishing inheritance tax would be a vote-winning but expensive option, and it should only be entertained if we can make the sums work elsewhere. Her preference is for no change or to increase the levy, to keep the public finances in good shape.

It's time to make your next decision.

DECISION

Abolish inheritance tax. You agree with Polly. You've seen for yourself the upset inheritance tax can cause and you predict many people would welcome its abolition. It'll punch a hole in the public finances, but you're confident you can still make the numbers add up and it feels like the right thing to do. *Record your decision in your Budget scorecard, noting its £7 billion cost.* Now turn to p. 208.

Make no change. You're happy with inheritance tax as it stands. *Record your decision in your Budget scorecard, noting no impact on the public finances.* Now turn to p. 208.

OFFICIAL – SENSITIVE

DECISION

Increase inheritance tax to 60 per cent. You agree with June. Inheritance tax is a levy that raises important revenue which you can spend on valuable public goods such as schools and hospitals, so why not raise some more? Stories like that of your constituent are regrettable, but the tax ultimately serves the greater good. *Record your decision in your Budget scorecard, noting the £4 billion gain.* Now turn to p. 208.

CHAPTER 23

The Motorist Dilemma

You can do an explicit deal with the tabloids.
You ask: what do you want to give me a good
headline on the day after Budget Day?
Philip Hammond

The big Budget decisions are now coming thick and fast, and the next one on your mind is a political hot potato: fuel duty. It's one of the government's significant earners – it raises nearly £25 billion annually, about 2 per cent of all tax receipts – yet it's also a levy that chancellors like to keep frozen for fear of angering the nation's approximately 30 million motorists. This is a point impressed on you by the editor of the *Sun*, one of the most read and influential papers in Britain, as part of a series of meetings you have with newspaper editors in the build-up to the Budget. Polly has arranged these in No. 11 so you can glad-hand the media titans who'll be deciding the all-important front pages and headlines after your big day.

'Our readers expect nothing less,' the *Sun*'s editor says of a fuel duty freeze, helping himself to a luxury cupcake in your study. The cakes were Polly's idea. ('It's not bribery,' she'd insisted. 'We just want to make sure everyone's in a good mood.') 'The country's already paying far too much tax as it is,' he says. 'Fuel duty would be the last straw. Freeze it or we'll give you hell.' Polly gives him another two cupcakes on the way out.

You're then reviewing the costings around fuel duty in the Treasury the next day when you note something unusual: your officials say you'd get no benefit from letting the tax rise with inflation. You ask: why not? Sir Alex lowers his head and inhales, as if preparing to explain something he's had to explain many times before. He says the problem is that chancellors before you always said their freeze on fuel duty was temporary, and hence the OBR assumes that fuel duty will rise at the next Budget.

'So it's been baked into their numbers all along that you're going to let fuel duty rise,' Sir Alex says. 'It's already in your surplus. If we want to maintain the freeze, it'll cost us about £5 billion.'

June's view is that you shouldn't go for the freeze. She's just met some economists from the Institute for Fiscal Studies, one of the UK's top think tanks, who made this case. They say it's a silly fiction in the Treasury's numbers that fuel duty is always assumed to rise, but never does. They say an increase in fuel duty in line with inflation is long overdue. June adds that there's the environmental impact to think about too – your government is trying to encourage people to use more public transport, so it's no bad thing if driving a car becomes more expensive – and she's also not sure we have an easy £5 billion lying around.

But Polly is adamant that you should maintain the freeze, no matter how costly or polluting it may be. She warns that a fuel duty hike would overshadow everything else in the Budget and guarantee negative headlines.

'You heard the *Sun*,' she says. 'They'll never let us get away with it.'

You look to Sir Alex for guidance. He concurs that Polly's analysis is indeed how chancellors before you have viewed this question, hence the repeated freezes, yet June's position is also valid.

'It's always a thorny one,' he says. 'And now it's up to you.'

It's time to make your next decision.

DECISION

Freeze fuel duty. You agree with Polly. You're wary of undermining your Budget by including a measure that's likely to spark a significant backlash, especially when you've had such an explicit warning from a key tabloid. It's an expensive move with a dubious environmental impact, but it will help voters with the cost of living. *Record your decision in your Budget scorecard, noting its £5 billion cost. Now turn to p. 212.*

Let fuel duty rise. You agree with June. You've only got limited funds at your Budget and this feels like a giveaway you can't afford. It's about time fuel duty went up after years of being frozen. You'll also be removing a dishonesty from the Treasury's calculations and doing right by the environment. *Record your decision in your Budget scorecard, noting the zero cost. Now turn to p. 214.*

OFFICIAL – SENSITIVE

YOU FREEZE FUEL DUTY

Polly thanks you with an exaggerated bow and says she'll be straight on the phone to the *Sun*.

'We want to get maximum mileage out of this,' she says. 'Excuse the pun. They'll be delighted. It's a real momentum-builder for the Budget.'

The front page of the next day's *Sun* does indeed make for enjoyable reading, with the splash dedicated to the exclusive news that you're set to extend the fuel duty freeze, accompanied by a photoshopped picture of you giving a big thumbs-up at a petrol pump. The paper is claiming it as a victory for their 'Keep It Down' campaign, and the leader column is effusive.

'*Sun readers will be delighted to see today's scoop that the chancellor is set to heed our campaign and freeze fuel duty at the Budget*,' it says. '*This is brilliant news and a testament to the power of this paper's influence. We thank you as ever for your support.*'

Polly is even happier when the story then leads the major TV and radio news bulletins for the rest of the day and also appears at the top of rival news websites such as *MailOnline* and the *Guardian*.

'We wouldn't have got this much exposure for it if we'd just waited to announce it with everything else on Budget Day,' she says. She also commissions immediate polling to see how the prospect of a fuel duty freeze is going down with the public, and the data you get back shows a bump in your approval ratings.

'Expertly done, chancellor,' she says. 'That was worth every penny.'

Add two points to your approval rating.
Now turn to p. 216.

YOU LET FUEL DUTY RISE

Polly drains her coffee cup and looks into it blankly for a moment. You ask if everything's okay.

'Yes,' she says. 'Absolutely fine. I'm just wondering how we sell this to the media. It's gonna be tricky.'

After some thinking, Polly says constructive ambiguity will be best. 'Telling the papers outright that we're hiking fuel duty, or even considering it, would mean we'd have the *Sun* on our backs every day until the Budget,' she says. 'Better to just shut up shop, decline to comment, and hope the bad news gets buried among everything else on the big day.'

Polly happens to get a phone call from a *Sun* journalist later that evening when you're together in No. 11, a call she takes while giving you a smile. You can hear the reporter is pushing for an exclusive and is asking directly about fuel duty.

'Fuel duty?' Polly says. 'You know how it is, old chap. We never comment on speculation ahead of the Budget. I genuinely can't give you a steer either way. Everything is still on the table. But rest assured, once we've made a positive decision about fuel duty, the *Sun* will be the first to know.'

Polly seems pleased with herself when she hangs up.

'Did you hear what I did there?' she says. 'I didn't lie. Once we've made a *positive* decision, I said I'd tell them. And we've made a negative one. So I guess they'll never know. Well, until they find out on Budget Day.'

Polly crosses her fingers and makes the sign of the cross. 'And then we pray.'

Now turn to p. 216.

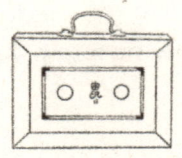

Taxing Wealth

Tax rates need to be competitive with other countries.
Norman Lamont

You're getting deeper and deeper into your Budget planning and the latest proposal on your desk is an intriguing one: a wealth tax targeting Britain's richest. An oft-discussed idea that polls well with the public, it's a policy that could raise significant revenue for the Treasury, but you're also aware it's politically risky if not handled sensitively. You invite Sir Alex, Polly and June into the No. 11 study to discuss the prospect further.

'Chancellor, you'll notice we've taken particular care with our policy design,' Sir Alex says, laying out a selection of documents before you. 'There are many pitfalls to avoid.'

Sir Alex explains what he and his Treasury officials have in mind: a one-off 5 per cent tax on people's wealth above £5 million, to be paid to the government in yearly instalments over a decade. Sir Alex says the tax would be paid by about 80,000 people, making up 0.1 per cent of the population, and is estimated to generate about £5 billion a year for the next ten years, for a total of £50 billion.

'Why only one-off though?' Polly asks. 'Couldn't we make it permanent? And why let them pay over ten years?'

Sir Alex says a one-off tax avoids many of the problems normally associated with wealth levies, namely that permanent wealth taxes incentivise the rich to either leave the country, disperse their assets among their family as gifts, or stash their wealth away in offshore tax havens.

'By immediately announcing a one-off wealth tax and applying it, it becomes very hard to escape,' Sir Alex says. 'And giving a decade to pay the tax bill is a show of reasonableness. Even the very wealthy may not have the cash to hand to suddenly pay a large sum to the state. Often their wealth is tied up in assets like property, companies and land.'

June appears to be cautiously in favour – you sense the design of the tax has appeased concerns she'd normally raise about the reaction of the wealthy – but she questions whether the benefit of the tax would show up in your budget surplus. 'For the purpose of the fiscal rules, don't the OBR only give us credit if a tax measure is permanent?' she asks.

'Yes,' Sir Alex says. 'Ordinarily they do. However, I've already spoken with their economists. They're indicating they'd be willing to make an exception here. Especially since the payments will be coming in over a decade.'

You turn to Polly for her thoughts, expecting her to support a policy that is seen by many as one of the fairest ways for the government to collect revenue. Instead, she seems unsure, chewing her pen tip with a frown.

'It would play well on the doorstep,' she says. 'But there's just one small problem. Mr Mann.'

A look passes between you and Polly and you twig the source of her alarm. Richard Mann, a high-profile philanthropist and one of the country's wealthiest people, is also a major political donor of yours and has contributed significantly to you and your party in recent years. Only last night, Polly was telling you of Mr Mann's intention to donate millions of pounds to the upcoming general election campaign, funds that would bankroll waves of targeted online advertising, reams of party political pamphlets and fleets of battle buses to ship activists to key constituencies, a veritable war chest that could be the difference between victory and defeat. But he'd also told Polly his plan to donate was strictly conditional on 'absolutely no funny business in the Budget'.

'I fear this may amount to funny business,' Polly says, scanning the documents with concern. 'Maybe I can smooth his feathers after the event. But it's a risk we should bear in mind.'

You feel indecision in the air and Sir Alex, June and Polly turn to you. It's time to make your next decision.

DECISION

Impose the one-off wealth tax. You think it's fair to ask the wealthiest to make more of a contribution to the public finances. It might upset some powerful people, but you're confident it will be well received by voters. *Note the £5 billion gain in your scorecard. Now turn to p. 220.*

Don't impose the wealth tax. While an attractive prospect, you're wary of upsetting the wealthy, and not least one of your own major donors. You feel the politics is too fraught and don't want to rock the boat. *Record your decision in your Budget scorecard, noting no impact on the public finances. Now turn to p. 222.*

OFFICIAL – SENSITIVE

YOU IMPOSE THE WEALTH TAX

You hold further meetings with Polly and June in No. 11 in the following days to harness your communication plan for the wealth tax, highlighting the sensitivity of the tax's design and pre-empting the expected attacks from your political opponents. But one such meeting is interrupted when Polly's phone rings.

'Speak of the devil,' she says, standing up to take the call. 'It's Richard Mann.'

Polly's face immediately loses its colour and you can hear shouting on the other end of the line.

'Photo?' Polly says. 'What photo?'

June is scanning social media and hands you her phone with a grimace. You see that a blown-up photograph of a woman carrying a set of notes into No. 11 is going viral online, the words '5% wealth tax' and 'comms plan' unmistakably visible. A snippet of the woman's watch and bracelet can also be seen, and they're obviously Polly's.

'Looks like the chancellor is planning to soak the rich …' is the caption accompanying the photo online, which has already been reposted thousands of times.

'You see, Ritchie, I'd been meaning to call,' Polly says, an exasperated hand to her forehead. 'I know what we said about no funny business. But I thought you'd be understanding.'

Polly's gaze is vacant as she then struggles to get a word in, as Mann monologues bitterly about the ingratitude of this government and especially you, the chancellor, after all he'd contributed over the years. When the call finally ends, Polly is despondent.

'That couldn't have gone much worse,' she says.

Unfortunately, the finer details of your wealth tax plan weren't visible in the photograph, meaning your political adversaries start putting out wild speculation about what you have in store, speculation which the Treasury press office struggles to quell.

Matters deteriorate further when Mann gives an exclusive interview to the *Telegraph* criticising your economic steward-ship, saying you're pursuing a vindictive agenda against the rich and that punitive taxes on the wealthy are the road to ruin. The main opposition parties seize on the Mann inter-view and run a series of online attack ads against you – the favoured line is 'Ritchie doesn't trust them anymore, so why should you?' – and your party HQ refuses your request to push out counter ads in response.

'Apparently there's now a big hole in the election finan-cial planning,' Polly tells you, who's still kicking herself over her carelessness with the Budget plans. 'So funds are being redirected.'

The punchy backlash from Mann and the accompany-ing political fallout keep the press occupied for at least a few days, with the various positive voices who support a wealth tax being largely drowned out by the spectacle of friendly fire and division. It makes for an uncomfortable period of sustained scrutiny that casts a shadow over your Budget plan-ning and it shows up in a hit to your poll ratings.

Deduct two points from your approval rating.

CHAPTER 25

A Controversial Guest

For the highest skill at the Exchequer does not lie
in calculations, but in judgments of all kinds.
Denis Healey, Chancellor of the Exchequer, 1974–9, quoting
twelfth-century treasurer of England Richard FitzNeal

Budget planning is continuing apace but you've also still got your busy schedule of chancellor meetings and public engagements as the big day nears. And it's one of those meetings that becomes a surprise point of controversy which sends Polly into a panic. It's your long-scheduled sit-down with the founder and CEO of one of the world's biggest e-commerce companies, who's visiting from overseas and is known to be mulling a major investment in Britain.

'We have to cancel the meeting,' Polly says, holding up a copy of that day's *New York Times*. 'The optics are too bad.'

You read the *New York Times*'s reporting, a deep-dive investigation exposing various human rights abuses across the company's supply chains, with suggestions of the extensive use of child labour and people trafficking. The CEO is quoted in the piece saying he'll do everything he can to establish what went wrong, but the paper also has a 'smoking gun' email showing the boss had been alerted to these practices months earlier and had done nothing.

'This guy is toast,' Polly says. 'There's no way you should be shaking his hand.'

Various left-wing journalists clock that you're due to meet the CEO and an online campaign swiftly emerges urging you to boycott him and the company. June is sceptical, however. She notes the CEO still owns more than 50 per cent of the business, meaning he has majority voting rights and hence can't be forced out by the board or its shareholders.

'You may think he's toast,' June says to Polly. 'But he'll survive this. And it's him and his firm that we want to invest in the UK.'

'Do we really still want this investment, though?' Polly asks.

'Of course,' June says. 'Have you seen the state of the economy? We'll take any help we can get.'

You thank them both for their advice and call in your diary manager. It's time to make your next decision.

DECISION

Go ahead with the meeting. You agree with June. It's deeply regrettable that this company has been involved in these practices, but it's your job to be hard-nosed and do what's best for the British economy. You're keen to do everything you can to secure this investment, and snubbing the CEO certainly won't help. If you choose this option, turn to p. 226.

OFFICIAL – SENSITIVE

DECISION

Cancel the meeting. You agree with Polly.
As much as you'd like to see more jobs created
and more investment flowing into Britain,
you still have your principles and your limits.
You also fear the political backlash if you're
seen to be turning a blind eye to what this
company has done. If you choose this option,
turn to p. 229.

OFFICIAL – SENSITIVE

YOU GO AHEAD WITH THE MEETING

The CEO's private car slows to a crawl as it approaches the gates of Downing Street, obstructed by a mob of photographers plus a sizable throng of protestors. It's those protestors you can hear as the CEO exits his vehicle and walks towards you – the chant is 'Morals not money! Morals not money!' – before he shakes your hand in front of No. 11. You lead him upstairs to the state drawing room. As you begin your discussion, the protest outside is still audible.

'Very sorry about all this razzmatazz,' he says. 'I made an honest mistake. We'll fix it.'

Your talks go well. The CEO appears receptive to your arguments about why he should consider Britain for his next investment location and you stress that you're ready to open any doors or grease any wheels if that would help make up his mind. Polly, who sits silently beside you throughout with hands clasped in her lap, visibly relaxes when he leaves.

'I really hope that was worth it,' she says. 'The papers aren't going to be pretty.'

You do indeed get a pasting from the media for taking the meeting – they choose from adjectives including 'spineless', 'unethical', 'weak', 'pliant' and 'shameless' to describe your conduct – but June reassures you it will turn out for the best.

'No-one will be saying that when this has all blown over and we've got tens of thousands of new jobs across the country,' she says.

You're with June and Polly in the No. 11 flat the following evening, sharing a well-earned drink after another hard day of Budget planning, when your phone lights up with an incoming call from the CEO.

'Here we go,' June says. Polly pours herself another glass of red wine. You put the call on speaker.

'Chancellor, thank you so much for welcoming me to Downing Street yesterday,' the CEO says. 'It was truly a privilege. I wanted to update you on our investment situation. We have made our decision.'

June gives you a wink.

'This really is an exciting time for our company. We are ready to make our next big commitment to Europe. And so … we've decided to invest in France.'

There's a moment of stunned silence. June looks at you in shock. You're still thinking of what to say when Polly grabs the phone and holds it to her chin, her other hand swilling her wine.

'Look *mon frère*,' she says. 'We never wanted you anyway. You can take your human-rights-abusing blood money and shove it up your —'

June's swift salvaging of your phone and speedy hang-up prevents the CEO from hearing the entirety of Polly's recommendation. Polly's invective continues for some time, finding increasingly fruity adjectives for the CEO and lamenting that her advice was ignored. Her mood only deteriorates further when the press gives you a fresh kicking over the investment decision.

'*It really is quite embarrassing to see our chancellor treated like a doormat in this way,*' is the verdict of the *Spectator*. '*If you're going to cuddle up with undesirables and invite them into the heart of the British government, you best be sure you're getting something in return. And yet here our chancellor has been left empty-handed and humiliated.'*

Deduct two points from your approval rating.
Now turn to p. 230.

YOU CANCEL THE MEETING

'We should publicise this straight away,' Polly says. 'Get the keyboard warriors off our back.'

Your cancellation of the meeting is welcomed in the left-wing media, but others take a more critical view. One prominent right-wing commentator accuses you of engaging in student politics and says you should've prioritised the economy and the national interest over grandstanding on human rights. Your principled stance does nothing to create jobs for the unemployed or raise living standards, they argue.

Criticisms of you deepen in the following days when the CEO announces the destination for his company's next major investment: France. Journalists ask whether he'd been considering the UK as an alternative and he says yes, he had, but your refusal of a meeting was decisive in what was a close call.

'Clearly Britain isn't ready for us, and that's fine,' the CEO says. 'We found the French to be far more welcoming.'

This prompts another wave of negative press coverage – 'Chancellor's Backfiring Boycott' is the headline of choice – and your political opponents paint you as naive and a block on British prosperity.

'This one I don't feel so bad about,' Polly says, reviewing the papers with you. 'Sometimes principles matter more.'

Deduct one point from your approval rating.
Now turn to p. 230.

CHAPTER 26

Taxing Vice

*I was under compulsion to advance an
environmental argument or a health argument.
Whereas what I wanted was the revenue.*
Norman Lamont on the sin taxes

There are just a few weeks to go until the Budget and it's an
unseasonably warm October day in Westminster, so you treat
your aides and senior officials to an upmarket catered picnic
in the Downing Street garden, a part thank you for everything
they've done, a part morale boost for the final hard yards
ahead. You notice Polly enjoying herself – liberally offering
the English sparkling wine and regaling colleagues with her
big post-Budget holiday jet-set plan to Mauritius. Polly brings
in her wine glass from the garden and is mid-elaboration of
her travel itinerary as you settle in the No. 11 dining room for
your afternoon Budget meetings.

'It's time to decide on another important area of taxation,' Sir Alex says, interrupting Polly and giving her a
pointed look over his spectacles. 'The so-called sin taxes.
We're considering duties on alcohol, sugary drinks, flying,
tobacco and vaping.'

Polly blushes as the table's attention turns to her. She sets down her glass and removes her vape from the table.

'Of course,' she says. 'Rightly so.'

Sir Alex shares a memo. It explains that these levies collectively raise almost £25 billion a year – about 3 per cent of all tax revenues, more than enough to fund the entire policing budget for England and Wales. The most lucrative for the Treasury is alcohol duties, raising £12 billion, followed by tobacco duties, which raise £9 billion. Sir Alex draws your attention to how you might increase these taxes further.

'We think we could raise another £3 billion,' he says. 'We'd do another 10 per cent on beer, wine, cider and spirits duties. For example, the duty on a pint of beer would go from 57p to 63p. The duty on a bottle of wine would go from £2.61 to £2.87. And so on. Altogether, that gets us £1 billion. Then another £10 on air passenger duty. That's a further £1 billion. And the rest comes from tobacco and vapes.'

June speaks up. She says she's in favour. She reckons we need as much revenue as we can get at this Budget and you can also sell these tax rises as being in the interests of both public health and the environment. 'Making vices more expensive through tax is like giving people a little economic nudge in the right direction,' she says.

But Polly disagrees. She says now is actually the time to be cutting these taxes. Doing so would win favour with the great British public who happen to quite enjoy a summer holiday abroad, a tipple and maybe even the occasional cigar.

'Not that I'm biased or anything,' she says, raising her glass. 'All good things in moderation, right? Let's not be killjoys. The press would love it too.'

Sir Alex points out the tax-cutting option. At a cost of £3 billion, you could reduce alcohol duties by 10 per cent, scrap the reduced rate of air passenger duty – a £7 tax on a basic economy ticket – and also make smoking and vaping cheaper.

'It's the tabloids' Budget dream,' Polly says. 'We should give it serious thought.'

The attention around the table turns to you. It's time to make your next decision.

DECISION

Increase the sin taxes. You agree with June. While perhaps unpopular, these taxes are generating important revenue for the Treasury and you'd like to squeeze out some more. You also recognise the potential positive social impact. If you're making things like drinking, smoking and flying less affordable, you're more likely to push people into healthier and more eco-friendly choices. *Record your decision in your Budget scorecard, noting the £3 billion gain.*

Make no change. You're happy with the rates of sin taxes as they are. *Record your decision in your Budget scorecard, noting no impact on the public finances.*

Cut the sin taxes. You agree with Polly. With an election just around the corner, what better way to curry favour with the public than by making the good things in life a little more affordable. It'll mean less money for the Treasury, but those will be more pounds in voters' pockets. And no doubt they'll raise a toast to you down the local pub. *Record your decision in your Budget scorecard, noting the £3 billion cost.*

CHAPTER 27

Helping the Vulnerable

*The process by which we drew up the
Budget was torturous.... This was no way
to run a raffle, never mind a Budget.*
**Alistair Darling on his difficulties preparing
for the Budget in spring 2009**

A key part of your pre-Budget work is to meet with business owners and employees who will be affected by your decisions, an opportunity to hear first-hand from the economic front-lines of Britain about what you can do to help. It also makes for a pretty good photo opportunity. So, with Budget Day drawing ever closer, you spend an afternoon touring your local high street accompanied by a TV crew and photographer, shaking hands here, listening to concerns there, genuinely interested in people's views as to what you should do. But your walkabout takes a dramatic turn when a scruffy man who'd been dozing on a bench approaches, shouting obscenities and gesticulating wildly. Your protection officers close ranks yet you indicate for them to step back. The photographer is snapping away and the TV camera is at your shoulder. Your calm response has a disarming effect on the man, who also appears surprised by the sudden media presence and boom microphone hanging from above. He looks up at it before speaking.

'Chancellor,' the man says. 'Why are you here? Don't pretend you care about us. We all know you politicians are all the same.'

You explain the purpose of your visit, conscious of the growing crowd and the rolling TV camera. Polly is stood out of shot behind the man gesturing for you to end this exchange immediately. You ignore her. You ask the man to tell you more about himself, and also what he'd like to see in the Budget. Asking a question has a further disarming effect and by now the man appears almost relaxed. He explains that he spent decades working in the steel industry before serving in the British military in Iraq and Afghanistan. He says he's struggled to find work since his overseas tours due to various medical problems, and is currently unemployed and living off Universal Credit.

'You've got to help us out, chancellor,' he says. 'I'm no skiver. Far from it. I've worked hard all my life. But things are tough right now. Universal Credit keeps me going.'

The exchange ends up leading the evening TV bulletins – 'Chancellor Ambushed' is the strapline on BBC News – and sparks a conversation among Britain's talking heads about welfare spending. Do we spend too little or too much? Should the chancellor increase Universal Credit at the Budget? Or perhaps it needs to be cut? This is a conversation that you continue with your officials in the Treasury the next day.

'You can go either way with it, chancellor,' Sir Alex says, handing you a briefing note on welfare spending. 'I warn you, however, that this is a sensitive issue.'

You read that government spending on Universal Credit, along with the legacy benefits it is designed to replace such as housing benefit and child tax credits, is about £80 billion annu-ally, almost the size of the entire education budget. Available to those who are out of work, unable to work, or on a low income, the standard monthly allowance for Universal Credit is about £400 for someone who is single and aged 25 or over. That figure is topped up if someone has children, a disability or a health condition.

Attached to Sir Alex's briefing note you see a Budget submission from a group of social justice think tanks and poverty campaigners, urging you to increase Universal Credit by £20 per week. At a cost of £4 billion to the Treasury, they say this would help 4 million of the lowest-income house-holds by £1,000 a year each and would lead to an immediate reduction in poverty. Almost one in five people in the UK lives in absolute poverty, they note, meaning their income is 60 per cent lower than the median income in 2010/11.

'It's certainly the compassionate option,' Sir Alex says of increasing Universal Credit. 'Though not without political ramifications.'

The alternative option put to you is to cut Universal Credit by £20 per week, generating £4 billion in savings. For once, Polly and June are both unsure in their advice. Polly says she can see the political merits of a Universal Credit cut – many people still see welfare as handouts to the lazy and a waste of their hard-earned taxes, and making the payment more generous could worsen unemployment because there'll be less incentive for people to go out and find jobs. But she's also worried about the potential backlash given your high-profile encounter with the military veteran.

'The left-wing press would lose it,' she says. 'It would look heartless, a total slap in the face for our man.'

June is similarly on the fence. She's all in favour of measures that improve our fiscal position, but she's wary of balancing the books on the backs of the most vulnerable. She says the economics around welfare spending are complicated. Having a reasonable safety net is good for helping people bounce back into employment because it avoids any downward spirals that might otherwise occur. But if the safety net becomes too generous, as Polly points out, that can have undesirable economic effects.

'This is one where I'm glad I'm just the advisor,' June says. 'Over to you, chancellor.'

It's time to make your next decision.

DECISION

Increase Universal Credit by £20 a week.
You're concerned about the ongoing levels of
poverty in Britain and want to do something
about it. You're aware of the stigma around
welfare and how this move will be criticised
in some quarters as yet another handout for
the undeserving poor, but you also know it will
genuinely help some of the most vulnerable
in society. *Record your decision in your Budget
scorecard, noting the £4 billion cost.*

Make no changes. You're satisfied with the
level of Universal Credit as it is. *Record your
decision in your Budget scorecard, noting no impact
on the public finances.*

OFFICIAL – SENSITIVE

DECISION

Cut Universal Credit by £20 a week.
You worry that welfare spending has become excessive in Britain and you want to remedy that. You fear the state's generosity is inadvertently contributing to higher levels of unemployment, and you want to free up resources to spend elsewhere at the Budget. You also expect parts of the tabloid press will welcome this move given the stigma around so-called benefit scroungers. *Record your decision in your Budget scorecard, noting the £4 billion gain.*

OFFICIAL – SENSITIVE

CHAPTER 28

Payroll Pressure

*My central problem was to discover which of the
decisions open to me as Chancellor were most
likely to get these people to behave as I wanted.*

Denis Healey on the workers and managers in British industry

You're coming to the end of your revolving door of Budget
consultation discussions and your final gathering is a breakfast meeting in 11 Downing Street with the heads of all of
Britain's major business lobbying groups. The Confederation
of British Industry, the British Chambers of Commerce, the
Institute of Directors, Make UK, the Federation of Small
Businesses ... together they represent the breadth and depth
of the UK economy and are a regular source of advice and
suggestions for your Budget. The conversation has turned
to National Insurance – a payroll tax, one of the Treasury's
biggest revenue-raisers – and whether employers should be
made to pay more. You lean forward and listen closely: this is
one of the options mooted by your officials and you're keen
to hear the feedback.

'Chancellor, you'll know better than anyone how important it is to maintain a competitive corporate tax regime,'

one of the business chiefs in a three-piece tailored suit says, sipping orange juice and nibbling on an almond croissant. 'National Insurance rates are already too high as they stand. Any further increases would deter job creation because it becomes too expensive to take on extra staff. If anything, jobs are likely to be cut and some firms would have to close.'

This view is met with much head-nodding around the table.

'You've got to give businesses a break,' another of the chiefs says. 'They're already struggling with higher energy costs, upward wage pressure, the difficult economic environment. Thriving companies are the backbone of the economy and they need a leg up, not even more burdensome taxation.'

Polly is hoovering up the leftover pastries with you after they've gone and her verdict is deep scepticism.

'The turkeys aren't going to vote for Christmas, are they?' she says, mouth full of *pain au chocolat*. 'They're literally paid to tell you that taxing business is bad. Big corporates are flush with cash, aren't they? I say we make them pay more.'

You run over the numbers on National Insurance with June in your Treasury office later that day. The government's second-largest source of revenue behind income tax, National Insurance raises about £170 billion, approximately the size of the budget for the Department of Health & Social Care. It's one of the big levers you can pull to raise revenue: just a 1 percentage point increase in the main contribution rate paid by employers would net you an extra £10 billion. June explains this is because of how far-reaching the tax is.

'Think about every major business in every corner of the country – the supermarkets, the retailers, the cinemas, the leisure centres, the banks, the hairdressers, the restaurants, and so on – all having to pay more tax to the government per person they employ,' she says. 'It quickly adds up.'

She says she sympathises with the views expressed at the morning roundtable. 'What you do as chancellor can have a significant effect on business confidence,' she says. 'Go too far on corporate taxes and you risk doing more harm than good. A vibrant economy is as much about encouraging the so-called animal spirits of entrepreneurs and business owners,' she says, 'incentivising them to take risks and be rewarded for their efforts. Every time we take more money from them, we discourage that.'

'It's like plucking the golden goose,' she says. 'If we pluck too aggressively, it will squeal. Or worse, run off.'

You thank June for her advice. It's time to make your next decision.

DECISION

Increase the main rate of National Insurance contributions for employers by 1 per cent. You agree with Polly. You want to generate extra funds for public spending, tax giveaways elsewhere or to boost your economic position, and this would be a major windfall for the Treasury. You acknowledge June's point about maintaining a business-friendly environment, but you think this is a tax rise that corporate Britain can shoulder. *Record your decision in your Budget scorecard, noting the £10 billion gain.*

Make no change. You recognize June's point about the dangers of too much taxation for businesses and fear pushing it too far. All in all, you're satisfied with the current level of National Insurance contributions for employers.

OFFICIAL – SENSITIVE

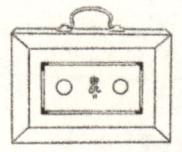

CHAPTER 29

Operation Stardust

There was even a secure zone in the
Treasury marked by white tape.
Roy Jenkins, Chancellor of the Exchequer, 1967–70, on the
stresses of preserving the confidentiality of the Budget

With the Budget now only a fortnight away, a key moment
has arrived: your receipt of the OBR's final economic forecasts that confirm the surplus at your disposal for the big day.
And while normally a picture of calm, the stress of this occasion is visible on Sir Alex's face: the brow deeply furrowed,
the glasses removed and polished with unusual frequency,
his wispy hair hand-combed again and again into the neat-
est of partitions. He's told you of previous horror stories
where chancellors have had awful final forecasts from the
OBR, throwing their entire Budget up in the air and requiring a root-and-branch rethink. Hence his trepidation as he
opens the OBR's file now. He studies it with a frown and then
slumps into his chair.

'It's excellent news, chancellor,' he says. 'Only the most
minor tweaks to the OBR's growth projections. We are as
we were.'

Relief washes across the room of gathered officials, many of whom are battle-hardened veterans of Budgets past. The civil servant manning the scorecard emphatically hits 'enter' on the surplus figure you've been working with, which is met with a mini cheer. But then it's straight back to work: Sir Alex asks that anyone who isn't cleared to discuss Operation Stardust to please leave the room immediately. Everyone departs except yourself, Polly, June, Sir Alex and two of the most senior civil servants.

'Remind me,' you hear Polly whisper to June. 'Which one is Stardust?'

Operation Stardust, a codename ginned up by Sir Alex and known only to a select few people in the Treasury, as is customary during the Budget process to preserve secrecy and reduce the potential for leaks, is your potential income tax cut, June tells Polly. The most eye-catching and newsworthy option drawn up by your officials, you know that this is perhaps the biggest call of your Budget, not least because of the prime minister's personal interest in the matter. And with the OBR's confirmation of your surplus, you can now see with clarity whether it's affordable.

Before making your decision, Sir Alex proposes going over the specifics of the proposal. He begins by reminding you of the current rates of income tax levied at different levels.

Band	Taxable Income (£)	Tax Rate (%)
Personal Allowance	Up to 12,570	0
Basic Rate	12,570–50,270	20
Higher Rate	50,271–125,140	40
Additional Rate	125,141+	45

You're considering a 1 percentage point reduction in the basic rate of income tax – paid on salaries between £12,571 and £50,270 – from 20 per cent to 19 per cent. For someone earning £35,000, it would mean a saving of about £220 annually.

'A nice pre-election giveaway,' Polly says. 'Couldn't we also cut the higher and additional rates?'

Sir Alex says that these are of course possibilities, but that your officials have focused on the basic rate cut because it's the move that would benefit most people. 'There are approximately 29 million basic rate taxpayers in the UK, compared to 5.6 million higher rate payers and 860,000 people who pay the additional rate,' he notes.

'And it's expensive enough as it is,' he says, citing the £7.5 billion price tag.

Notwithstanding the obvious political benefit from the tax cut, your officials caveat that reducing the basic rate is not the most efficient way to help the poorest households. Someone earning £50,000, for example, would get an extra £370 from the change, whereas someone earning £20,000 would only get an extra £74.

'It's rather ineffective at addressing inequality,' Sir Alex says. 'If inequality happens to be our concern.'

June's view, as it's been throughout, is that affordability matters most. She says you should only cut income tax if the sums add up.

'There's no point putting more money in people's pockets if we also trigger a market crisis because the public finances are in chaos,' she says. 'We aren't winning any elections in that world.'

Later that afternoon, you meet the prime minister in the Cabinet room, a long-scheduled appointment to nail down the big policies of the Budget in light of the OBR's final forecasts. The prime minister's enthusiasm is almost puppy-like when you start with income tax.

'Come on, chancellor,' she says. 'Give me the good news. We're doing this, right?'

It's time to make your next decision.

DECISION

Cut the basic rate of income tax.
You're convinced of the need for an eye-catching pre-election tax cut to win over voters. It may be expensive, but it's the kind of big, bold, easy-to-understand gesture that will capture the electorate's imagination and give you a healthy boost in the polls. It's also what the prime minister desperately wants, and she's the boss after all. *Record your decision in your Budget scorecard, noting the £7.5 billion cost.* Now turn to p. 250.

OFFICIAL – SENSITIVE

DECISION

Make no change to income tax. As much as you'd like to announce a headline-grabbing tax cut at the Budget, your first responsibility is to maintain order in the public finances and this is one giveaway too far. You agree with June that pushing ahead with unaffordable tax cuts risks a dangerous market reaction, and avoiding that matters more than appeasing the prime minister. *Record your decision in your Budget scorecard, noting no impact on the public finances.* Now turn to p. 252.

OFFICIAL – SENSITIVE

YOU CUT INCOME TAX

Emily claps her hands together and does a little jig.

'I knew you'd deliver,' she says. 'Never in doubt. The election's all but won.'

You talk her through the rest of your Budget policies but you sense she's not really listening, still high on the thrill of the income tax cut. You reach the point of explaining the minutiae of your decision on the level of public spending when Emily puts a hand on your shoulder and says: 'It's going to be great, chancellor. You've done a brilliant job.'

You discuss the prime minister's reaction in your No. 11 flat with Polly and June later that evening, as you share a celebratory takeaway pizza to toast the OBR's beneficence and your imminent tax cut for the nation.

'Happy wife, happy life,' Polly says, mouth full of pizza. 'Or in this case, happy prime minister, happy ...'

'Yeah, it doesn't work,' June says.

Polly is nevertheless just as excited and says you've got the best possible rabbit to pluck from the hat on Budget Day. She says she will keep said rabbit in a high-security hutch under 24-hour surveillance and it will never, ever escape. She runs through who knows about the policy: you, the prime minister, Sir Alex, herself, June and two Treasury officials. She says she's personally read the Riot Act to the civil servants and the Treasury *omertà* is strong, so she's confident there'll be no leaks.

'It's just our little secret,' she says, eyeing you and June, running an imaginary zip across her mouth. 'And what a secret it is.'

Polly's phone rings. She says it's the BBC. She rejects the call.

'That reminds me,' she says. 'Chancellor, I need to ask you something.'

Now turn to p. 254.

YOU DON'T CUT INCOME TAX

'What do you mean we can't?'

The atmosphere is suddenly very tense between you and Emily. She's pulling her frowning, calculating face, the same face she pulls when she responds to the leader of the opposition at Prime Minister's Questions or when she's dealing with a civil servant she doesn't rate. You explain that you've gone through the numbers carefully and an income tax cut isn't feasible at this moment. You can almost see the cogs whirring as she decides what to say next. You sense she's teetering between hostile confrontation and begrudging acceptance. Something changes behind her eyes and she slides into the latter.

'That's very disappointing,' she says, looking down at the Cabinet table. 'I really thought we could make it happen. But as I always say: I trust your judgement, chancellor.'

Your established career in politics has made you a veteran of interpersonal diplomacy and interpreting what people really mean from what they say, and the disingenuousness in the prime minister's final statement was unmistakable. You're used to Emily speaking with such conviction, yet those last words were worryingly hollow.

You run her through the rest of your Budget measures but she seems disinterested, still stewing on the lack of the income tax cut. She stops you when you get to the finer points of your public spending decision, saying that she's sure you've prepared the right package and that you have her full support.

'Full support?' Polly asks in the No. 11 flat later that evening, as you're sharing a celebratory Chinese takeaway along with June to mark the OBR's gentle final forecasts. 'Surely that goes without saying, doesn't it? Bit weird that she put it like that.'

June says it sounds like the prime minister was sulking.

'Not without reason,' Polly says. 'A tax cut would've been very nice. But we are where we are.'

Polly is interrupted by her phone ringing. She says it's the BBC. She rejects the call.

'I think I know what that was,' she says. 'Chancellor, I've been meaning to ask you something.'

Now to turn to p. 254.

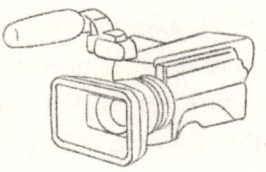

CHAPTER 30

Facing the Music

*The chancellor probably ought to be a
bit distant from the media.*
Norman Lamont

Polly explains that the nation's broadcasters have been pestering her because they want you to appear on the Sunday morning breakfast shows the weekend before the Budget. She says it's a media appearance that chancellors have typically done in years gone by, though others have sometimes decided to skip it.

'And that would be my advice,' Polly says. 'The interviewers are just going to ask you over and over again variations on "What's in the Budget?", and you'll say they'll have to wait and see, and it will go back and forth, back and forth, and then the press will go wild writing things like "Chancellor refuses to rule out income tax cut" and "Chancellor raises prospect of abolishing inheritance tax", and whatever other fantastical pet projects they have. They'll also probably put together a package of you refusing to answer a Budget question five times in a row and it will look shady and evasive. Better to just send out the chief secretary and be done with it.'

June, however, takes a different view. She says you should do the interviews and use the opportunity to set out the big picture for your Budget and prime the public for what's to come. She says you can politely but firmly say you won't be able to answer about specific measures in your Budget speech, but you're happy to talk generally about the economy and what's at stake for the country. 'You want to project confidence and competence, and doing the interviews would achieve that,' she says.

'We shouldn't pass up the chance to speak to the nation,' June says. 'Budgets are a major moment and we should communicate our approach clearly.'

It's time to make your next decision.

DECISION

Do the media broadcast round. You agree with June. You feel comfortable facing the press and want to secure some more publicity around the Budget. You're ready for any hostile questioning and want to use this chance to explain your broader thinking about the decisions you're about to unveil. If you choose this option, turn to p. 258.

OFFICIAL – SENSITIVE

DECISION

Skip the media broadcast round. You agree with Polly. You've seen how these pre-Budget media appearances can go for a chancellor, and you'd rather avoid the awkward confrontation and don't want to fuel any wild press speculation that might come from the interviews. The media will learn soon enough what's in your Budget – they can wait just a few more days. If you choose this option, turn to p. 261.

OFFICIAL – SENSITIVE

YOU DO THE BROADCAST ROUND

You have to squint under the bright glare of the studio lighting as your interview begins the following Sunday, one of the BBC's top political journalists sitting across from you with a pad full of questions and a wily gaze.

'Chancellor, thank you so much for joining us this morning,' she says. 'There's so much to get through, so let's get straight into it. The Budget's next week. People up and down the country are looking to you for help at what is a very difficult time. We all know that an election is imminent. So, let me ask you directly. Can we expect a cut to income tax?'

You keep a deliberately straight face and say that, while you'd love to come on the programme and reveal your entire Budget, unfortunately everyone will have to wait for your appearance in the House of Commons on Wednesday to hear the specifics. And, you say, you'd be more than happy to come back on the show after your Budget to discuss it in full. You're just about to continue with your big-picture explanation on the economy when the interviewer cuts you off.

'Sorry, chancellor, that won't do,' she says. 'Millions of people watching this programme want to know right now what the government, what you, are going to do for them. We all know the cost of living has been painfully high. Times are hard. People deserve a cut in income tax, don't they?'

You maintain your straight face and congratulate the interviewer on their artful attempt to get you to reveal the contents of your Budget, but you repeat that you cannot comment either way on specific measures. However, what you can talk about is the bigger picture facing the economy and that's why—

'Chancellor, forgive me for interrupting,' she says. 'I'm not asking you to reveal your Budget at all. I'm simply asking do people *deserve* a cut in income tax?'

You reply that the interviewer is in fact trying to get you to talk about specific policies that may or may not be in the Budget, and you simply won't be drawn on any of it.

'So the hard-working people of Britain *don't* deserve a cut in their taxes, that's what you're saying?'

Again, you politely but firmly say that you won't be commenting on specific tax measures, no matter how enterprising or carefully constructed the question may be. This draws a long-held and pronounced frown from the interviewer, who leans forward on her pad of paper and clasps her hands.

'Chancellor, I'm going to give you one last chance,' she says. 'I'm very clearly not asking you to reveal any of the specifics of your Budget. I simply want your view on a general point: do the people of Britain *deserve* an income tax cut?'

· · ·

Polly is scrolling her phone with a scowl later that afternoon as she reads the write-ups from the morning broadcast round, your exchange on income tax with the BBC having made the biggest impression.

'Chancellor REFUSES to Rule Out Income Tax Cut in Potential Budget Bonanza,' says the *MailOnline*. ('Didn't I predict this exact headline!?' Polly asks.)

'Quids In! Chancellor Set to Cut Income Tax after Admission in BBC Interview,' reports the *Daily Express*. ('What admission?!' Polly asks.)

'WATCH: Awkward Moment Chancellor Clams Up on Income Tax,' reports the *Daily Star*. ('Clams up!' Polly says. 'Since when was speaking in reasonable and intelligent sentences of English clamming up!? I knew this was a bad idea. Just knew it.')

June is more positive, however. She says she thinks you handled yourself well and, despite the tough lines of questioning, you landed lots of your main talking points across the various interviews that morning. She says the alternative – going into hiding and not speaking up for your Budget – would've looked worse.

'Chin up, Polly,' June says. 'We're almost there.'

Now turn to p. 263.

YOU SKIP THE BROADCAST ROUND

You tell Polly that you'd like Simon to take your place.

'Wise move,' she says. 'I'll tell the Beeb.'

You think that's the end of the matter, but Polly comes back to you and says the BBC are insisting it's you. She says the other broadcasters are making the same demand and are threatening to empty-chair you otherwise.

'An empty chair would perhaps have more charisma than Mr Miser,' Polly says. 'But it's a look we'd rather avoid. I'll tell them you've got an unavoidable diary clash and they need to grow up and therefore it has to be the chief secretary.'

Alas, Polly's ploy fails and the BBC's flagship Sunday politics show before the Budget opens with the camera slowly zooming in on a guilty-looking empty black chair, the presenter expressing their deep disappointment that the chancellor has chosen to avoid media scrutiny at this critical moment for the nation.

'Who knows what gremlins the chancellor has in store for us on Wednesday?' the presenter says, the camera still zooming. 'If only we could've asked. Viewers will have to make up their own minds about this chancellor and this government's attitude to accountability.'

The rest of the media piles in too, commentators accusing you of running scared of legitimate questioning and calling your absence an affront to openness and democracy.

'We can't win, can we?' Polly says, scrolling the Internet with mild dismay later that afternoon. 'Put ourselves at the mercy of a pre-Budget broadcast round and get shredded for not answering any questions, or avoid said ordeal and be told we're missing in action. Let's just hope we get a fairer hearing from the press on Budget Day.'

Deduct one point from your approval rating.
Now turn to p. 263.

The Final Days

*Once I had taken the final decisions
and the die was cast, a quiet peace descended.*
James Callaghan

Perhaps counterintuitively, your stress levels decline in the final days before the Budget because so much of it is settled. Your major policy measures went into the OBR a fortnight earlier and your Budget speech has been all but complete for at least a week. June's taken the lead on running a fine-tooth comb over the minor measures in the Budget – the policies that have a negligible economic impact in the eyes of the OBR, but nevertheless make up much of what you'll announce in your near-hour-long speech – because it's here that chancellors before you have slipped up. Making a small tweak to VAT to apply it to hot snacks such as sausage rolls and Cornish pasties, for example, was a minor measure that stole the headlines for the wrong reasons at George Osborne's Budget in 2012, triggering a wave of negative coverage about the so-called 'pasty tax'. June says it's her sworn mission to root out anything that has the air of a pasty tax.

'It's going to be good vibes only,' she says, tapping the ancillary cache of documents that will be published alongside your Budget. 'Pots of money for road improvements. Backing for new bridges and infrastructure. Extra funding to renovate high streets in marginal constituencies. Consultations on bright ideas from the City and business. Absolutely no bedbugs.'

Polly is on jokes duty and periodically interrupts you in the No. 11 study as you're practising your speech to test out her latest gags. Most of her suggestions are at the expense of the prime minister, and you suggest she might better redirect her humour at the opposition for fear of personal consequence.

'Of course, chancellor,' she says, saluting. 'Best not bait the boss.'

On the day before the big event, you have a practice run with your fellow Treasury ministers for the traditional Budget photo, sorting out the order in which you'll come out of the door of No. 11 and who will stand where when you raise your famous red box to the world's cameras in Downing Street. You feel a bit silly rehearsing the line-up and the gesture, but Sir Alex insists there'd be nothing worse than you and your ministerial team coming out in a disorganised muddle just hours before your Budget.

'We want to at least give the impression that we know what we're doing and we're all singing from the same hymn sheet,' he says with a wink. 'Can't make it too easy for the tabloids.'

You also have a very special engagement on the afternoon prior to the Budget: a personal private audience with the king at Buckingham Palace. It's a reminder of what the 'HM' stands for in 'HM Treasury' – His Majesty's – and how, under Britain's constitutional monarchy, at least in a ceremonial sense, the government, and therefore you, ultimately serve at the pleasure of the king. He greets you warmly in a grand, stately room, complete with antique gilt mirrors, a white marble clock and decadent floral bouquets. You talk him through all of the big Budget announcements and are struck by his depth of understanding on politics and economics.

'That's what you get from a head of state,' Polly says, when you share the generalities of your chat with her and June afterwards, though you studiously avoid breaching the confidence of a meeting that is always strictly private. 'The monarch's seen it all. But wait. You told the king everything? Even our most top-secret decisions on tax?'

Yes, you reply, you did. As is expected.

'Calm yourself,' June says to Polly, seeing her panic. 'It's the King of the United Kingdom we're talking about. I doubt he's got the *Sun* on speed dial. The rabbits are safely in their hutch.'

You join your aides and key officials for a takeaway pizza in the No. 11 dining room that evening – scene of much of your policy planning, a fitting location for a jovial last supper – and then retreat to your study for a final read-through of your speech and the main Budget documents before they're printed. This is a crucial logistical exercise all of its own: as you're heading to bed for some much-needed rest ahead of the chancellor's equivalent of Christmas Day, they're firing up the printers at a secret location to produce physical copies of your fiscal plans, accompanied by trusted Treasury civil servants who are on hand to make any last-minute changes. The confidentiality and security of the whole process are vital. Many a financial trader or plucky journalist would love to get their hands on those documents and the market-sensitive information they contain. The share prices of so many companies – tobacco makers, pub chains, major retailers, construction firms, banks, and so on – have the potential to change based on your taxation plans, movements that will bolster or deplete investment portfolios. The value of the more-than £2 trillion of UK government debt – much of it made up of interest-paying bonds held by pension funds which are providing retirement incomes to millions of Britons – is also in the balance. Even the value of pound sterling itself is subject to move. Hence the secrecy of the Budget documents is paramount. So, as you tuck yourself under the covers, you imagine that secure vehicle racing across London in the early hours of the morning while the country slumbers, weaving past the taxis and the freight lorries, stopping at traffic lights, covertly carrying the precious bundles of what you've toiled over for months now, that little red book of the Budget which will be revealed to the world in just a few hours' time. A Budget to shape the fortunes of the nation. This is it. One more sleep.

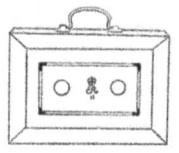

CHAPTER 32

B-Day

The waiting time until 3:20 … felt almost endless.
Roy Jenkins on his Budget of 1968

You wake energised for the day ahead, glad the time has finally come to share all the ideas and economic secrets you've been holding in your mind for weeks. You take a hearty breakfast – Sir Alex had warned you that opportunities to eat today will be very limited, so best tuck into your Weetabix – and go down to the No. 11 study for a final rehearsal of the speech. Polly and June soon join you. Polly says she's barely slept from the nerves and excitement, ideas for gags still coming to her in the small hours. She says she thinks she should become a comedian. June, who looks perfectly well-rested and poised, says the world of politics could never afford the loss. June then says she's checked the newswires from overnight and fortunately there's no need for any last-minute additions to the opening of your speech – no condolences to be offered to the victims of a domestic disaster or conflict, no sporting success to be congratulated, no international economic ruction needing mention. There's also no sign of any Budget morning leaks in the papers, much to Polly's delight.

'It's Watership Lockdown,' Polly says, casting an approving eye over the front pages. 'The maximum-security hutch remains a fortress.'

It gets to mid-morning and you walk through No. 11 to No. 10 for the Cabinet meeting. Normally the prime minister takes centre stage at this gathering, but today the focus is on you. You brief your fellow ministers in broad strokes on what's coming in the Budget, deliberately leaving out the juicier details to avoid any last-minute leaks.

With Cabinet complete, you head back to No. 11 for the traditional Budget Day photo. You file out into Downing Street with your fellow Treasury ministers and hold the famous red box aloft. There'd been some debate between Polly and June as to whether you should smile in this photo. With the world's media calling out for your attention – 'Over here, chancellor! Just this way, chancellor!' – you decide on a look of assured optimism. It's a moment of significant pride for you. All those years you've spent striving to make a difference in public life – winning your seat in Parliament, building a network of support, rising through the ministerial ranks – and now here you are, posing in a photo for the history books, your friends and family no doubt watching on proudly at home. The red box in your hand – first made for Gladstone around 1860 and used for the majority of the next 150 years until its final presentation by George Osborne in 2010 – now has a modern replica, and it contains your Budget speech. Polly had double-checked on this point, seeking to save you from the fate of George Ward Hunt, Disraeli's chancellor in 1868, who is said to have arrived at the House of Commons for his Budget only to open his red box and realise he'd left the speech behind. Once you've adequately shown off your red box to the gathered throng of photographers, you pace along Downing Street into your waiting ministerial car, ready to whisk you over to Parliament for the big event. The nerves are starting to jangle.

**You're now only a few moments away
from delivering your Budget.**

**If you decided to cut income tax, turn to Chapter 33
on p. 270. If you decided not to cut income tax,
turn to Chapter 34 on p. 274.**

CHAPTER 33

Run, Rabbit

If what you have is big enough, it doesn't really matter if the press finds out, if your reforms are still going to change the course of the country.
Jeremy Hunt

Your Jaguar has barely left the black gates of Downing Street when your phone vibrates with a BBC breaking news alert. Your stomach falls.

Exclusive: Chancellor to Cut Income Tax in Major Pre-Election Giveaway

The Chancellor of the Exchequer will announce an income tax cut as the centrepiece of today's Budget, a bold pre-election giveaway that would save the average earner hundreds of pounds a year.

The chancellor, who is due to present the Budget in the House of Commons shortly, is expected to reveal a 1p cut in the basic rate of income tax, according to a senior government source.

> The tax cut, devised in conjunction with the prime minister, will be painted by the chancellor as a reward for hard-working Britons and only possible due to the government's measured stewardship of the public finances.

You're about to read further but up pops an incoming call from Polly. Normally she's travelling with you in the car, but she and June are heading to the Commons on foot.

'My rabbit!' she says. 'What a disaster. Who's the leaker!?!'

Sir Alex is beside you and is also reading the article. He pushes his spectacles to the end of his nose and holds his phone at arm's length.

'I fear she's done it again,' he says. 'Our senior government source. The most senior of them all. *In conjunction with the prime minister.* That's a rather telling clause.'

Polly seizes on the theory and has a little meltdown about the injustice of it all – why couldn't she let you have your moment? Why does she always have to take credit? What is a Budget without its bunny? – but you have little time to digest the implications because your car is pulling up in Parliament. You go to brief the whips – they're the ones responsible for maintaining party discipline and they'll be encouraging your MPs to give you vociferous support in the chamber during your speech – before you head to your parliamentary office behind the Speaker's Chair, and it's here you take a final breather as the clock ticks closer to midday. Polly and June give you some last words of reassurance and support – June has calmed Polly a modicum about the rabbit escapee, but you sense she's still furious – and then you're entering the House of Commons, greeted with an almighty cheer from your benches. You take your seat next to the prime minister, who's about to start her 30-minute Prime Minister's Questions (PMQs) session, a warm-up to the Budget.

'I can't believe it leaked,' she whispers, without turning to you. 'Oh well. Even more publicity for us.'

PMQs goes by in a blur, the atmosphere in the chamber a mixture of excitement and impatience for your main event. The leak of the income tax cut has had an electrifying effect on the benches behind you, your MPs buzzing at what you're about to announce, and a depressing effect on the benches opposite, your political opponents grimly calculating what it means for the election. At last, PMQs winds up and you gather your notes, palms sweaty.

'I call the Chancellor of the Exchequer!' the Speaker says.

You rise to a full-hearted roar, surveying the occasion with a confident smile. All things considered, delivering the Budget speech is one of the easier parts of this whole process – you've read out many a tract in your political career, after all – but it's nevertheless gratifying to hear Polly's jokes land and your MPs murmur approvingly in all the right places. You end up speaking for almost an hour, longer than Disraeli's shortest-ever Budget speech of 45 minutes in 1867, but positively brief compared to Gladstone's 4 hour and 45-minute oration of 1853. You spy the briefest glimmer of hope among the opposition as you appear to conclude your remarks with no income tax cut in sight ... but then trigger the biggest cheer of the day when you say you have one final thing to announce.

Your ears are ringing with acclamation when you sit down, your MPs waving their order papers in delight, the prime minister slapping you on the back and saying how brilliant you'd been. The leader of the opposition rises to answer you – a tough gig given they have to respond to your measures on the fly and normally it's the shadow chancellor who speaks on economic matters – and you bat away their criticisms with a re-emphasis of the generosity of your tax cut. You leave the chamber to more cheers from your MPs and return to your parliamentary office, where June and Polly are already waiting.

'So,' you ask them, the adrenaline still flowing and your heart racing. 'How did that go?'

It's time to check the market reaction to your Budget.
If your final surplus, taking into account your Budget
measures, is 0 or higher, turn to p. 286. If your
final surplus is negative, turn to p. 279.

CHAPTER 34

The Phantom Rabbit

*The Chancellor of the Exchequer's is a lonely job
... when he is obliged to disappoint the hopes of his
Party and the aspirations of his colleagues – not to
speak of his own. Without the support of the
Prime Minister, it is impossible.*

Denis Healey

Your car is arriving at the black iron gates of Parliament when
your phone vibrates with a BBC breaking news alert. You're
stunned by what you read next.

> **Exclusive: Chancellor Blocked Prime
> Minister's Income Tax Cut in Dramatic
> Budget Talks**
>
> In an extraordinary case of division at the top of the
> British government, the BBC can reveal that today's
> Budget was due to include an income tax cut devised
> by the prime minister, but the plan was dramatically
> blocked at the eleventh hour by the chancellor.

The public were due to be in line for a 1p cut in the basic rate of income tax, saving the average earner hundreds of pounds a year, until the Treasury intervened, according to a senior Downing Street source.

'The PM was all for it but the chancellor got cold feet,' the source said. 'And it's left the Budget threadbare.'

Budget discussions between No. 10 and No. 11 are normally strictly confidential, hence the significance of today's revelation. The news will pile extra pressure on the chancellor, who is due to unveil the Budget in the House of Commons shortly.

You're about to read further but you're interrupted by an incoming call from Polly. She unleashes an impressive barrage of swear words before saying anything intelligible.

'What traitors,' she says. 'How could No. 10 do this to us? Who would've briefed this?'

Sir Alex is alongside you in the car and says the precise identity of the source is irrelevant.

'It's either the prime minister herself or someone speaking with her blessing,' he says. 'It's just as bad either way.'

Polly launches into a Machiavellian analysis of the leak. She thinks the prime minister is doing some combination of: self-preservation in case the Budget bombs; setting you up so she can sack you before the election if the polls aren't looking good; petulant vindictiveness for defying her over the tax cut; taking you down a peg so that you're less of a threat for the leadership in any post-election power struggle.

'Actually, I'd say it's all of those things,' Polly says.

But you barely have time to process the story because now you've parked up outside the Commons and you're heading inside for your last-minute Budget preparations. You go to speak to the whips – they're responsible for maintaining party discipline and they'll be encouraging your MPs to make an approving din during your speech – before you head to your parliamentary base behind the Speaker's Chair. The scene in the whips' office was a little troubling when you arrived, the chief whip clearly engrossed by the BBC's article and hastily shutting it down when you poked your head around the door. You take a moment to huddle with June and Polly before entering the House of Commons chamber, Polly still shaking her head.

'I can't believe what she's done,' she says. 'She's ruined it for you.'

You walk into the House of Commons at 11.59am, greeted with hearty cheers from your own benches on your right, but also boisterous jeering from the opposition MPs on your left. The jeering grows louder as you take your seat next to the prime minister, who's just about to start her 30-minute session of Prime Minister's Questions (PMQs), a sea of mocking parliamentarians pointing between you and your leader.

'I've no idea where that story came from,' she whispers, without turning to you. Before you can reply, the Speaker is calling the first question and the prime minister is on her feet at the despatch box. It requires all your effort to keep a straight face during the next half-hour, your mind racing with the leak from No. 10 and what it means for the reception of your Budget. At last, the Speaker calls 'final question' and you shuffle the notes of your speech in preparation. You sense most MPs have barely been following this question-and-answer session with the prime minister, a mere aperitif to the main course of your Budget, but they're attentive now. Your own MPs give you an almighty roar when the Speaker says 'Chancellor of the Exchequer!' and you rise with your stomach a pit of nerves.

What makes the speech so difficult – notwithstanding the regular heckles of 'Where's the income tax cut, chancellor?' and 'Does the prime minister agree with you, chancellor?' – is that you dread its conclusion. During the speechwriting, you and your team had done your best to backload all the friendlier policies to build to a rousing finish, but you now know that's all going to sound hollow compared to the phantom rabbit of cutting income tax. You end up speaking for an hour – Polly had joked you should try to beat Gladstone's record of 4 hour 45 minutes from back in 1853 – and the final moments are just as bad as you'd feared. Most of the noise is coming from the opposition benches when you finally take your seat, your political opponents gleefully waving their order papers and continuing to point between you and the prime minister. Emily makes a show of heartily slapping you on the back as you sit down – 'brilliant, chancellor, brilliant' – but the parliamentary sketch writers later say it's as if she was delivering those blows with a knife.

'The chancellor wants us to believe that this is the best economic plan for Britain,' the leader of the opposition says as he begins his response, eyeing you cruelly. 'But why should the public believe that, when it isn't even believed by the prime minister?'

Cue raucous cheers and more mocking laughter. Once again, it takes a heroic effort to keep a straight face. It feels like an eternity before you can finally get away from the chamber, your initial interrogation by MPs complete, and the prime minister disappears without speaking to you. You take refuge in your parliamentary office and find Polly and June waiting. Polly's demeanour is crushed.

'You did your best, chancellor,' she says. 'That was horrible.'

You thank Polly for her support and turn to June. You're aware that Parliament is just one theatre of importance on Budget Day, and hence ask her how it went down in the City.

It's time to find out how your Budget has been received on financial markets. If your final surplus, taking into account your Budget measures, is 0 or higher, turn to p. 287. If your final surplus is negative, turn to p. 279.

YOUR SURPLUS IS LESS THAN 0

'Not looking good,' June says, frowning at her phone. 'Gilt yields spiking. The pound falling. It's early days, but this is far from ideal.'

June says the immediate commentary is around the OBR's verdict that you've breached your fiscal rules. 'People were expecting us to push the envelope ahead of an election, but not to this extent,' she says. She reads out the snap verdict from an analyst at Goldman Sachs:

> The chancellor's Budget has thrown caution to the wind and left the government tearing up its key fiscal targets. Given the plans announced today, there are major question marks around this administration's commitment to economic stability. We expect the chancellor's package to stoke inflation and force the Bank of England to raise interest rates. The government's borrowing costs are set to rise further and there is a strong possibility of UK debt levels spiralling out of control. In light of the looming general election and populist pressures on the government, we now have a risk-off view on the UK. Britain's fiscal stance suddenly lacks credibility and we doubt that the bond markets will react favourably.

You ask June to keep you posted every half-hour with the latest market movements as you continue your post-Budget routine. Next up is a series of sit-down chats with the political editors of the BBC, ITV, Sky, Channel 4, Channel 5 and GB News back in No. 11, and unfortunately those chats are dominated by discussions of the backlash in the City, no matter how hard you try to pivot back to the positives of your Budget.

'The pound is still falling and UK borrowing costs have risen past multi-decade highs,' the BBC's political editor says, a fact repeatedly thrown at you across each of the interviews. 'You've got this badly wrong, haven't you, chancellor?'

Your mind is distracted as you continue the day's formalities, doing a photo op at a local business before passing by the Two Chairmen pub near the Treasury to share a well-deserved drink with your civil servants. The mood is positive but you can't help but notice the worrying signs: the sly glances at mobile phones to check the latest on the markets, the overly earnest congratulations from people in the crowd, the notable absence of any of the senior staff from the financial stability team. You then head to a pre-arranged event in the City for another photo op at Bloomberg, the financial data giant, to discuss your Budget with some captains of finance, an engagement which feels like entering the lion's den. Polly was suggesting you cancel the event given the ructions on markets, but June said running scared would look even worse.

'These are the people who've been shorting the pound all day and advising their clients to dump gilts,' June says in the car on the way over. 'But we're going to shake their hands and stand tall anyway.'

The whistlestop tour of Budget Day then takes you to St Pancras station, where you hop on a train to Derby in preparation for the next morning's media broadcast round. Polly has picked out a factory as a suitable backdrop for your interviews, as you seek to convey the image of a chancellor in touch with the country and getting to grips with the economy. Just as your train is pulling out of London, you get a call from Sir Alex.

'Chancellor, you may remember my maxim about the undesirability of being asked to join a discussion with the Debt and Reserves Management team,' he says. 'Alas, we must break that maxim now.'

You dial into a call with your senior officials and the conversation is sobering. They say that the sell-off was still in full swing when markets closed and they expect it to continue in the morning. Their view is that any further decline in UK government bonds risks a vicious cycle, where Britain's increased debt interest payments further worsen our budgetary position, resulting in even less confidence in the UK's fiscal stance and even more selling of government debt, leading to even higher debt interest payments, and so on. Their suggestion is that you may wish to signal the potential for a reversal of your plans, to arrest the market slide.

'A U-turn is never particularly desirable,' Sir Alex says. 'But sometimes there is no choice.'

You call the prime minister when the discussion ends. The political drama of the day has been overtaken by the urgency of the financial fallout and you're keen to hear what she thinks you should do. She is unperturbed, however, saying it's nothing but a little wobble and it will all calm down eventually.

'We can't U-turn on the Budget, chancellor,' she says. 'People will think we're amateurs. Strong and stable, that's what I say.'

You go to bed that evening exhausted by the day's events and fearful of what will come next. Polly's counsel is that the prime minister is right and you should face down the City, show the speculators and the fat cats who is boss. She says we can't be letting overpaid bankers override the will of the democratically elected government. June has gone very quiet, feeling the same shellshock as you. You'd agreed over dinner that you'd hold the line for now, say you have full faith in your Budget and that you believe it's the best plan for Britain.

The first hour of the broadcast round the next morning goes as well as you might hope, Polly giving you the thumbs-up as you stoically defend your Budget and make as many references as possible to your best measures. But you know that the biggest test is coming at 8.10am. That's your interview slot with the BBC Radio 4 *Today* programme, a lengthy grilling with their top talent which is sure to involve a painful cross-examination on the state of the markets. They will have reopened ten minutes earlier. Indeed, the presenter begins with exactly that.

'Chancellor, thank you for joining us. As we speak, I'm looking at a graph on my screen. The pound is plunging once again. The cost of government borrowing is climbing remorselessly. There is no end in sight to this brutal rejection of your Budget by the markets. You're going to have to U-turn, aren't you?'

You gulp and repeat your carefully rehearsed line about how you have full confidence in your economic plans and that it remains the best approach for the country. The line sounded better when spoken in confidence with June and Polly.

'But how is any of this good for the country?' the interviewer asks. 'Banks are already repricing mortgages. That means immediate pain for homeowners, and house purchases will collapse. The weaker pound means going on holiday is now much more expensive. Prices will go up in the shops because it costs more to import goods from overseas. There's talk of an emergency intervention by the Bank of England. There's talk of you needing to go to the IMF for a bailout. You know all this, chancellor. Surely you can see this Budget is a disaster?'

You maintain your defence for an excruciating ten minutes – it feels more like an hour – before you hurry back to the train station to return to London. Polly spends the journey wincing at the Internet reaction to your Radio 4 interview, with every political pundit of note calling it a total disaster which has exacerbated the deepening sell-off. You get a call from the Governor of the Bank of England, who informs you that he's about to announce an emergency intervention to stabilise the situation.

'But we can't do this alone, chancellor,' he says. 'It might be worth a rethink.'

You're glad to return to the familiar surroundings of your study in No. 11 Downing Street, and you're heartened to see that the Bank's move prompts a relief rally in both sterling and UK government debt. You want to speak with the prime minister to strategise next steps, so you ask your private secretary to arrange a quick meeting. But he comes back and says the prime minister is unavailable until further notice. June raises her eyebrows.

'What could be more important than talking to you right now?' she asks.

You send Emily a message but it goes unread. Polly spends the rest of the afternoon fielding calls from journalists, telling them there will categorically be no change in your Budget plans.

'Look at the markets,' you hear her saying to one reporter. 'The situation is stable. The storm has been weathered. What was that? There's a rumour we're about to U-turn? I think you need better sources, mate.'

After a strange extended period of silence from No. 10 that lasts until the early evening, you finally get a knock on the door. It's the prime minister's chief of staff. He says she's ready to see you now in the Cabinet room. You're just about to get up and go when Polly curses.

'What on earth is going on?' she says, showing you her phone. It's an article in the *Financial Times*.

Exclusive: Chancellor to U-Turn on Budget after Market Meltdown

The government has decided to row back on its market-crashing Budget, with the chancellor expected to announce a dramatic reversal of its economic plans in the House of Commons tomorrow.

The decision to U-turn was made between the prime minister and chancellor in Downing Street today. The chancellor recognised the errors that had been made in the Budget and acknowledged a change of course is necessary, according to a senior No. 10 source.

'The Treasury has been kicking and screaming over this but the PM will always do what's right for the economy,' the source said. 'She convinced the chancellor to make amends. This is the chancellor's mess, after all.'

'We're being completely shafted,' Polly says.

You're still reading the article as you walk over to the Cabinet room. You enter to find Emily sat alone at the centre of the table, her demeanour icy. You demand to know what's going on.

'This is the meeting that's just been reported in the press,' she says, her tone transformed from the carefree air with which she spoke to you the previous evening. 'We are agreeing that a change of course is required. You will make a statement in the Commons tomorrow. And though I regret you feel the need to, I accept your resignation once that statement has been made. You have served me well as my chancellor. But I think we can both see that the end has come.'

You listen in disbelief. You barely recognise the woman you're speaking with, your long-time political ally who is now firing you with a steely gaze. Later, you'll begin to rationalise her decision – making you the scapegoat, salvaging any hope of winning the election by inserting a new chancellor and having you take the fall for everything – but in that moment, you're simply stunned. You try to find the words to fight but the feeling of betrayal and helplessness is too overwhelming. The prime minister says she'll be sure to give you a peerage in her resignation honours if you cooperate, and that she'll be the first person to champion your legacy if you resign on good terms.

'I'm sorry it's come to this,' she says, finally showing a hint of emotion. 'Unfortunately, there's no other way.'

You walk back to your study in a daze, dreading what the next few days will bring. The first humiliation of having to announce your Budget U-turn to a braying House of Commons, the second humiliation of then announcing your resignation, followed by the tearful goodbyes with your senior aides and the handing in of your red box. You'll be reading your own political obituary by this time tomorrow, the nation's commentators telling the tale of the chancellor who picked a fight with an unbeatable adversary: the bond market. Never again will you be as powerful as you are now, and you feel a sudden sadness. Your political career is over.

Commiserations! Your journey as chancellor has come to an end. Return to p. 153 to try again!

YOUR SURPLUS IS 0 OR HIGHER
AND YOU'VE CUT INCOME TAX

'It was brilliant, chancellor,' June says, checking the markets on her phone. 'Thumbs-up from the City. Gilts and the pound have taken it all in their stride. A few critical voices saying we could've given ourselves more headroom against the fiscal rules. But otherwise calm.'

You turn to Polly for her thoughts and she's ecstatic, says it couldn't have gone any better. 'Did you see their faces when you announced the tax cut?' she asks. 'Did you hear all those laughs for my jokes? Give me a stand-up show already.'

But there's little time for further self-congratulation. The urgent task of selling your Budget to the media and the public now begins, and Polly has arranged calls for you with each of the major national newspaper editors to make your case. First up is the *Sun*.

'Here we go,' Polly says. 'The verdict.'

It's time to discover the initial reaction of the press.
If you chose to let fuel duty rise, turn to p. 296.
If you froze fuel duty, turn to p. 291.

YOUR SURPLUS IS 0 OR HIGHER
AND YOU'VE NOT CUT INCOME TAX

'Pretty well, actually,' June says, checking the markets on her phone. 'Gilts and the pound both stable. Some are saying we've pushed it too hard against the fiscal rules, we should've left more of a surplus. But it's a minority view. The City is becalmed.'

'At least that's something,' Polly says, head still in her hands. 'I still can't believe it. Wait until I get my hands on anyone from No. 10.'

Feeling a bit better after the update from June, you prepare yourself for your next Budget Day engagement: phone calls with each of the nation's national newspaper editors. Polly had set these up in advance, a chance to sell your package directly to the people who'll be deciding tomorrow's all-important headlines. First up is the *Sun*.

'Well here we go,' Polly says. 'Let's hope we've caught him in a good mood.'

It's time to discover the initial verdict of the press.
If you chose to freeze fuel duty, turn to p. 288.
If you let fuel duty rise, turn to p. 300.

YOU FROZE FUEL DUTY
AND DIDN'T CUT INCOME TAX

'All a bit of a mess, isn't it chancellor?' the *Sun*'s editor says. 'Well done on fuel duty. But a dust-up with No. 10 on income tax? I'm afraid the splash writes itself.'

You do your best to encourage him to look past the theatrics of the day and focus on your Budget goodies, not least the fuel duty freeze, but he hangs up with a laugh.

'I'll do my job, chancellor, and you go back to trying to do yours,' he says.

Your calls with the rest of the editors go a similar way, the leaders of the British press clearly preferring the low-hanging fruit of political soap opera over the technical details of tax rates. You head back to No. 11 for some more media – sit-down broadcast interviews with the political editors of the BBC, ITV, Sky, Channel 4, Channel 5 and GB News – and each exchange descends into a tiresome back and forth over why you didn't cut income tax and whether you still enjoy the prime minister's support.

'Of course you still enjoy the prime minister's support,' Polly mutters darkly when the final interview ends. 'The more salient question is whether she enjoys yours.'

You find yourself distracted as you go through the motions of the rest of Budget Day – a photo op at a local business, a brief stop at the Two Chairmen pub to raise a glass with your exhausted Treasury officials who are in a celebratory mode, an event in the City at the financial data giant Bloomberg to discuss your package with some captains of industry, before heading to get a train northward for an overnight stay in Derby ready for the next morning's broadcast round. You're really worried about the front pages. You'd been hoping for some nice headlines on the more populist moves in your Budget – not least the fuel duty freeze – but you sense it's all been marginalised by the rift with No. 10. Your fears are confirmed when Polly shows you the early editions before you go to bed.

'PM & Chancellor at War on Day of Budget Drama,' declares *The Times*. 'The Income Tax Cut That Never Was,' says the *Independent*. 'Division!' is the simple verdict of the *Sun*, their splash a full-page picture of you sat beside the prime minister, both of you looking stern, with the image photoshopped to look like it's been torn in half.

'I've seen some rough Budget headlines in my time, chancellor,' Polly says. 'I regret to say this is up there.'

You do your best to retain your composure during the next morning's broadcast round as the questions continue about your non-existent income tax cut and relationship with the prime minister. Polly almost intervenes in your 8.10 interview on BBC Radio 4's *Today* programme – famously one of the hardest post-Budget media moments – because she's so fed up by the line of questioning, but luckily June holds her back and prevents what would've been an even bigger story.

'But why did they spend so much time on what isn't in the Budget rather than what is?' Polly asks afterwards.

It's a relief to return to No. 11 that afternoon, finally escaping the glare of the media and having a chance to take stock. June joins you with a cup of tea and says she's philosophical about the situation. She says the media circus around your tiff with the prime minister will soon abate, and that's when the press will have to start talking about your actual Budget measures. She says she's going to commission a focus group to see what the country really thinks about your package, and we should defer the post-mortem until those results are in.

'I'm still hopeful, chancellor,' she says. 'There's much we can be proud of in that Budget.'

And that's the dossier that June puts on your desk a week later, a qualitative report from the focus group accompanied by polling data.

'The people have spoken,' she says.

It's time to see how your Budget has been received by the public. Turn to p. 304 to read June's focus group and polling report.

YOU FROZE FUEL DUTY
AND CUT INCOME TAX

'Not bad at all, chancellor,' the *Sun*'s editor says on speaker phone, Polly silently fist pumping and doing a little dance. 'I can't say we love everything you've done. But your decisions on income tax and fuel duty will be music to the ears of our readers. You have our support.'

Your calls with the rest of the editors are similarly positive, notwithstanding a few gripes here and there – both the *Guardian* and the *Mirror* take you to task over not committing more funds to public services, and the *Telegraph* complains about the overall level of taxation even with your income tax cut – and so you finish your ring-round feeling a sense of relief. There's still plenty of time for your Budget to unravel, but the early signs are encouraging.

You head back to No. 11 for some broadcast interviews, successively sitting down with the political editors of the BBC, ITV, Sky, Channel 4, Channel 5 and and GB News, handling their questioning with ease because the subject matter is so well known to you after your months of intensive preparation. Then you head for a nearby photo opportunity, the setting deliberately selected to best illustrate your flagship Budget measure, and hence Polly has picked a thriving local business where you shake hands with employees who will benefit from the tax cut, hoping these photos will feature prominently in the papers. Then your aides accompany you to another Budget Day tradition – sharing a drink with your officials at the Two Chairmen, believed to be the oldest pub in Westminster and favoured watering hole for Treasury civil servants. The atmosphere is buoyant as your staff chink glasses and toast the Budget, the crowd spilling out onto the street and eager to catch you for a selfie. Then you're jumping back into your ministerial car to be driven over to an evening event at Bloomberg, the financial data giant, a nice photo op where you discuss your Budget with captains of finance and the City. You half-jokingly thank the gathered fund managers and traders for not shorting the pound or triggering a sell-off of UK government debt, which is met with a gale of laughter.

'The funny thing is, some of them will have been trying to do exactly that,' June says, as you're driving away afterwards, Polly licking her fingers from the tasty canapés. 'And you ruined their day.'

Your next stop is St Pancras station to catch a train heading north. Polly has arranged for you to do the following morning's broadcast round from a factory in Derby, and hence an overnight stay beckons. You check into the local Premier Inn and gather around Polly's laptop after some dinner to take a peek at the early editions of the next day's front pages. It's a warming sight: your income tax cut has indeed stolen the headlines, Britain's press leading on your giveaway and framing it as the de facto opening gambit of the election campaign.

'Chancellor Cuts Income Tax in Key Pre-Election Budget,' declares the *Financial Times*.

'More Cash for Britain's Strivers,' says the *Sun*, featuring a flattering picture of you giving your speech in the Commons.

'A Budget for Hard-Working Britain,' is the simple verdict of the *Daily Mail*.

'I'm proud of you,' Polly says, giving you a hug. 'A day to tell the grandkids about. But just don't mess it up tomorrow. We've come this far. I want you dazzling on the *Today* programme.'

You reassure Polly you'll do your best and wish your team good night, well aware that the job still isn't done. You may have lived and breathed this Budget to the point of memorisation of its finer details, but the rest of the country is only just learning about it – a fragment here on the radio news bulletin as they pick their kids up from school, a brief glimpse there of the top TV news headlines before they switch to their favourite show, an overheard comment in the pub as they catch up with friends. Your job of selling this package has barely begun, and in a few hours' time you're going to be beaming into kitchens and living rooms and people's cars on the morning breakfast shows to explain and defend what you've done. If anything, people's understanding of your Budget is more important than its actual contents, and it's that understanding which you'll try to shape tomorrow. You get into bed feeling a great sense of achievement and gratitude for how the day's gone, but also determined to not slip up now. Sleep comes quickly.

· · ·

Your wake-up call comes in the form of a 5am rat-tat-ta-ta on the door from Polly, who'd never normally be this sprightly at such an hour but who's still high on the positive press coverage.

'Come on, chancellor,' she says. 'Let's do this.'

The first hour of your broadcast round – clad out in hard hat and hi-vis vest on a factory floor – is a success as you flit between Times Radio, Sky, the BBC, LBC, taking every opportunity to pivot your answers to the tax cut and running down the clock by giving deliberately long responses focusing on the more generous aspects of your Budget. It's soon approaching 8am, however, and you know that the big one is next – the 8.10 interview on BBC Radio 4's *Today* programme. It's a famously tough and extended grilling from the BBC's sharpest interviewers, so if any hidden gremlins are going to be exposed or if you're going to be caught out on your defence of a controversial measure, it will be here.

'Chancellor, thank you so much for joining us,' you hear through your earpiece, trying to put out of your mind the millions of people who are listening to what you're about to say next. 'This Budget was a naked attempt to win the next election, wasn't it?'

The next ten minutes pass very quickly. You deny any motivation for your tax cut beyond doing what's best for the British people and economy, and nimbly hit your talking points when challenged on the more controversial decisions in your Budget. The interviewers try to interrupt you when you start taking liberties with your rambling answers on the virtues of cutting income tax, but you insist on finishing your points and succeed in whittling away many precious seconds. Polly gives you a round of applause when it's done.

'I could kiss you, chancellor,' she says. 'In fact, I will.'

You return to London and spend the rest of the afternoon surveying more of the Budget reaction from your study in No. 11. With every passing moment, the peril of your Budget unravelling seems to be abating. Nevertheless, you're eager to see some concrete evidence on how each of your policy decisions has landed with the public, and that's what June brings you in a dossier at teatime. She says she commissioned a focus group in Dartford, the UK's current longest-running bellwether political constituency. Whichever party has won Dartford has gone on to win nationally since 1964, making it an ideal place to take the temperature of the nation.

'Here we go then,' she says. 'The moment of truth.'

It's time to see how your Budget has been received by the public. Turn to p. 304 to read June's focus group and polling report.

YOU LET FUEL DUTY RISE
AND CUT INCOME TAX

'I was very clear, chancellor,' the *Sun*'s editor says with some menace. 'Punish the nation's motorists at your peril.'

You begin to point out the generosity of your income tax cut but he interrupts you.

'Robbing Peter to pay Paul then, aren't you, chancellor?' he says. 'We see straight through it. You should've listened.'

The call is worryingly brief and similar complaints come from the other national editors. The tax cut is welcomed but they worry you've given with one hand and taken with another. The *Guardian* and *Mirror* also have gripes about the level of public spending – '*surely you could've done more, chancellor*' – while the *Telegraph* is concerned that the overall tax burden is too high.

'Gosh they're hard to please,' Polly says, when your round of calls is complete. 'Don't they realise we have to make the numbers add up?'

Your post-Budget schedule continues with a return to No. 11 and sit-down interviews with the political editors of the BBC, Sky, ITV, Channel 4, Channel 5 and GB News. To Polly's great distress, each of those chats involves lengthy back and forths on the fuel duty hike.

'I feared this would happen,' she mutters darkly as you then head to a local business for a photo opportunity, taking snaps with workers in a bid to promote your tax hike. Next is another post-Budget tradition, a quick drink at the Two Chairmen pub, believed to be the oldest in Westminster and a favoured drinking spot for Treasury civil servants. The gathered crowd of officials is spilling out onto the street – their mood a mix of exhaustion and relief – and you pose for a few selfies, thanking them for all their hard work. Then it's off to the City for an event at the financial data giant Bloomberg, where you shake hands with captains of industry who congratulate you on your Budget and praise your stewardship of the public finances.

'If only the general public shared their appreciation of fiscal prudence,' June says sardonically. 'Though to be fair, I bet the cost of fuel is very far from the minds of the people we met tonight.'

Your final port of call in London is St Pancras station, where you board a train north to Derby for an overnight stay in preparation for the next morning's broadcast round. It's as you're checking into your Premier Inn that Polly shows you the early editions of the next day's front pages.

'Brace yourself,' she says.

'Chancellor's Fuel Duty Betrayal!' declares the *Sun*.

'Motorists Feel the Squeeze on Day of Budget Pain,' says the *Guardian*.

'Pain at the Pumps!' says the *Daily Mail*.

The next morning's broadcast round isn't much better, the questioning dominated by the rising cost of fuel as you struggle to bring the focus back to your tax cuts. The final nail in the coffin is your 8.10 interview on BBC Radio 4's *Today* programme, famously one of the trickiest post-Budget moments where you're grilled by their star interviewers. If a Budget is going to fall apart, there's a good chance it will happen in this interview.

'Chancellor, we all know that Budgets can sometimes unravel,' the interviewer begins, articulating the fear you'd shared with Polly and June the night before. 'With that one policy which overshadows everything else. Sparks an outcry. Turns the public against you. You'll have seen the initial reaction to your decision to hike fuel duty. Let us start with this: is your Budget unravelling?'

You say that no, of course it isn't, and that in fact your Budget did a lot of good in areas such as—

'But chancellor, you'll have seen this morning's front pages. Not a single positive headline. Our inbox has been flooded with listeners getting in touch saying you've got this wrong. That they're worried they won't be able to fill up their cars to go about their daily lives. Surely you're going to have to think again here, aren't you?'

What follows is an awkward and stilted exchange where you continually defend your decision and the interviewer replies by reading out successive irate emails from the public telling you to scrap the hike. You sense Polly wants to end the interview early – like a boxer's manager throwing in the towel – but June holds her back, knowing that being seen to run away would cause even more of a media spectacle.

You're glad to return to London that afternoon and retreat to the safety of your study in No. 11. June's verdict is that the furore around fuel duty will blow over by the weekend and that's when the rest of your Budget will get a fairer hearing. She says she's going to commission a focus group and some polling to see how it's all landed.

'The press make a lot of noise and think they're all-powerful,' she says. 'But what really matters is the view on the street.'

However, by the time June puts her focus group report on your desk a week later, the fuel duty situation has worsened.

Protests have sprung up around Westminster, the air filled with angry car horns. The *Sun* has been leading on the story every day since the Budget, finding ever more lurid anecdotes of people who say they'll suffer from a hike in the cost of fuel. You've had to answer an Urgent Question in the House of Commons on fuel duty tabled by the opposition, facing rows and rows of heckling MPs. Polly shares an old mantra about Budgets: if yours is still being talked about beyond the weekend, then something has gone badly wrong. You want the news agenda to move on swiftly to other matters. 'If only that would happen here,' she says.

'Let's not get too downbeat,' June says, opening the dossier from the focus group. 'Not before we've seen this.'

It's time to see how your Budget has been received by the public. Turn to p. 304 to read June's focus group and polling report.

YOU LET FUEL DUTY RISE
AND DIDN'T CUT INCOME TAX

'What a mess, chancellor,' the *Sun*'s editor says. 'A bust-up with No. 10 over income tax and a hike in fuel duty? It's one of the worst Budgets I can remember.'

You begin a defence but he speaks over you.

'Don't take us for fools, chancellor,' he says. 'You should've listened to the prime minister on income tax. And to me on fuel duty. I was crystal clear.'

The call ends abruptly and Polly is pale-faced. 'Let's hope the rest of the press see it differently,' she says.

Unfortunately, they don't. The unanimous verdict of the nation's newspaper chiefs is that both the fuel duty hike and the division with No. 10 are disasters that overshadow anything commendable in your Budget. This theme continues in the sit-down broadcast interviews you have with the political editors of the BBC, ITV, Sky, Channel 4, Channel 5 and GB News in No. 11 that afternoon. For all your attempts to hit your positive talking points, the conversations keep coming back to fuel and the psychodrama with the prime minister.

You put on a brave face for the rest of the day's engagements – a photo opportunity at a local business, the customary post-Budget drink with your officials at the Two Chairmen pub, an event in the City to sell your Budget to captains of industry, before taking a train north to Derby for an overnight stay ahead of the morning media round – but that only masks the dread you feel about the front pages. Polly is subdued too, and she hands you her phone as you're checking into your hotel.

'They're not for the faint of heart,' she says.

'Was That the Worst Budget Ever, Chancellor?' asks the *Sun*.

'Pain at the Pumps on Day of Budget Chaos,' says the *Guardian*.

'Infighting with No. 10, Motorists Whacked … It's an Omnishambles!' says the *Daily Mail*.

Your dread continues into the broadcast round the next day, which you do in hard hat and hi-vis from a local factory. You struggle your way through the first hour, gamely trying to draw attention to the better parts of your Budget, but with little success.

Then comes the media moment you've been fearing most, the 8.10 slot on BBC Radio 4's *Today* programme. If ever a Budget is going to fall apart, it will happen here, under the extended scrutiny of the sharpest interviewers. Though in this case, it feels like the unravelling is already in full flow.

'Chancellor, people are already calling this one of the worst Budgets in living memory,' the interviewer begins. 'Where did it go so wrong?'

You begin by contesting the interviewer's characterisation of the situation. You say there was much to welcome in your Budget, including—

'Chancellor, forgive me for interrupting. Surely you can see what a disaster this is? There's open division between you and the prime minister. Millions of motorists are up in arms because you've put up the price of fuel. I've never seen such a swift and decisive backlash against a Budget. Are you going to have to consider your position?'

You maintain your stoic defence for the next ten minutes – it feels far longer – and not even Polly has any words of reassurance when the interview ends.

'Well at least that's over,' she says.

You return to London that afternoon and take sanctuary in your study in No. 11. You've been asking for a meeting with the prime minister to confront her about the leak, but her chief of staff says she's unavailable until further notice. The Budget fallout spills over into the weekend papers and by Monday morning there's a full-blown motorists' protest blocking up Whitehall, the air filled with angry car horns and placards poking out of windows calling for you to scrap the fuel duty hike. On Tuesday, you finally hear word that the prime minister is willing to see you.

'Chancellor,' she says coldly, as you enter the Cabinet room. Emily is sat at the centre of the table, alone, and in front of her is an array of the last few days' front pages. The coverage has been damning.

'I'm sorry we've not been able to talk before now,' she says.

You sit across from her and demand she explains the Budget leak.

'That's not what I wanted to discuss,' she says. 'I wanted to talk about all this.' Her hand sweeps across the newspapers.

'I fear too many mistakes were made at the Budget. I made my misgivings known to you on income tax. Clearly you got it wrong on fuel. It puts me in an awkward position.'

It dawns on you then where this is going.

'I have to think about the election and what's best for the party,' she continues. 'I've sadly come to the conclusion that your presence has become less of a help and more of a hindrance. But with a fresh face, perhaps we still have a chance. And I'm grateful that you see it this way too. So yes. I accept your resignation.'

The words hit you like a hammer blow and for a moment you feel unsteady.

'I'm sorry it has to end this way,' she says, for the first time speaking with emotion. 'We've come so far together. But you know how it is. Politics is politics. It's nothing personal. And I'm glad you're taking the noble route of resignation.'

Your mind is racing as you stagger back to No. 11 after the meeting, still shocked by what just happened. The thought of what the next few days will involve is crushing: the ignominy of your resignation letter, the tearful goodbyes with your aides, the obituaries they'll write about you – the chancellor hoisted by the petard of their own Budget – and the sad realisation that you'll never again enjoy such power. It's slowly sinking in. Your political career is over.

Commiserations! Your time as chancellor has come to an end! **Return to p. 153 to try again.**

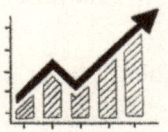

CHAPTER 35

The Public's Verdict

To see how your policies have been received, find the letters in the 'Result' column in Table A that correspond to the options you selected for your Budget. Then, find those letters in Table B and see the impact on your approval rating.

TABLE A

Policy Area	Options	Result
Public Spending	Cut by 1%	A
	Hold steady	B
	Increase by 1%	C
Inheritance Tax	Increase inheritance tax	D
	No change	E
	Abolish inheritance tax	F
Fuel Duty	Freeze fuel duty	G
	Let fuel duty rise	H
Wealth Tax	5% levy on wealth over £5 million, collected over ten years	I
	No change	J
Sin Taxes	Increase duties on alcohol, tobacco, sugary drinks, flying and vaping	K
	No change	L
	Cut duties on alcohol, tobacco, sugary drinks, flying and vaping	M
Welfare	Increase Universal Credit by £20 weekly	N
	No change	O
	Cut Universal Credit by £20 weekly	P
National Insurance	Increase National Insurance for businesses	Q
	No change	R
Income Tax	Cut the basic rate by 1%	S
	No change	T

TABLE B

Result	Focus Group Reception	Impact on Your Political Approval Rating
A	Participants in the focus group expressed concern about the impact of your spending plans on the quality of services in their local area, especially in the NHS and schools. 'I know it's not as bad as the papers were saying beforehand, but this is just austerity again, isn't it?' one said. 'I can't believe they think spending cuts is what this country needs right now,' another said. 'We should be investing more in public services, not less.'	−2
B	Stagnant public spending was viewed with some negativity in the group, with several people wondering whether the quality of services would deteriorate given growing demand in areas like health and education. 'I'd rather the government spent a bit more to be honest,' is the view of a single mother. 'I was waiting in A&E for hours to be seen just a few weeks ago,' says another lady. 'Surely the system needs fixing.'	−1
C	Your plan to boost spending was met warmly by the focus group, with participants expressing hope that the funding would translate into better public services. 'I think the chancellor's made the right call there,' says a young man. 'It's about time we put some proper investment into what matters: the nation's health, education, security.' Another man said they hope the money goes toward higher public sector pay. 'Nurses and doctors do so much for us, but they earn a fraction of what bankers get,' he said. 'It's only right that we recognise their social contribution.'	+2

Result	Focus Group Reception	Impact on Your Political Approval Rating
D	The majority view in the group was opposition to your inheritance tax hike, with participants picking up on the right-wing media's description of the decision as an 'increase in the death tax'. 'I'd rather the government got rid of it entirely,' one elderly gentleman says. 'I've been taxed on everything I earn all my life, and now they want to tax me even more a second time when I die? It's a disgrace.'	−2
E	N/A	0
F	Abolishing inheritance tax was well-received, with participants saying the new system would be more compassionate and fairer on those who are grieving for lost loved ones. Your personal anecdote about the case of your constituent also went down well, humanising the issue and making you appear in touch with the public.	+2
G	This was a popular decision. Participants expressed relief that you hadn't put up the price of petrol or heating oil at a time when living costs are already sky high. 'I don't think I could've managed if the cost of filling my van had gone up,' says a tradesman.	+1
H	This was a deeply unpopular decision. Everyone in the focus group was upset about having to pay more for fuel. 'I need my car for everything: going to the supermarket, taking my little one to nursery, commuting to work,' said one woman. 'And now I've got to pay more just to do my daily essential routine? It's ridiculous. Surely the government can find other ways to raise money than hitting ordinary folk like us.'	−3

Result	Focus Group Reception	Impact on Your Political Approval Rating
I	Your wealth tax received largely positive views in the group, with a majority saying that millionaires should definitely be paying more in tax. 'If you've got £5 million, you can spare 5 per cent for the rest of us,' said one young lady, who's struggling to get on the property ladder. However, a minority expressed misgivings about the tax, saying you were stoking the 'politics of envy' (the choice catchphrase pushed by one of one of the UK's most influential tabloids, whose proprietor will be hit by the levy) and making Britain less attractive for the wealthy. 'The chancellor says it's a one-off, but politicians lie all the time, don't they?' says one retired businessman. 'These things are never a one-off.'	+1
J	N/A	0
K	This decision went down badly in the focus group. Participants said times are tough enough as they are, so it makes no sense for the government to make it even more expensive to enjoy things like a drink down the pub with friends or a flight abroad. 'It's the nanny state, isn't it?' said one man. 'They want to price us out of what's good in life. But we still want to do those things. So we just end up poorer.'	−2
L	N/A	0

Result	Focus Group Reception	Impact on Your Political Approval Rating
M	This policy was warmly welcomed. The consensus view of the group was that people should be trusted to make their own decisions about the so-called vices, and the government's duty cuts would make a few of life's pleasures more affordable. Several participants said they were planning to go to the pub after the session and would raise a glass to the chancellor.	+2
N	This policy drew a mixed reaction from the group. A sizable minority said they thought it was wrong that more of their hard-earned money would be going to people on welfare, and that they wanted benefits to be cut to encourage people to get a job. But the rest of the participants were supportive, saying it was right to give more to the poorest to try to alleviate poverty.	+1
O	N/A	0
P	This decision divided opinion among participants. A vocal few said they were glad to see a cut to welfare, arguing it would incentivise people into employment and that it was right to re-direct their hard-earned taxes into more important things. But the rest of the group said they were uncomfortable with the decision. They said they feared it would push some of the most vulnerable into destitution, and that the government was failing in its responsibility to the poorest.	−1

Result	Focus Group Reception	Impact on Your Political Approval Rating
Q	The focus group was largely opposed to this decision. One dissenting voice said they were glad to see businesses paying more in tax, but the rest of the participants had misgivings. 'My business only makes a small profit and I employ five staff,' says one cafe owner. 'I'll have to let at least two people go because of this. The costs of running a business – whether its ingredients, energy, rent, insurance, wages – are already so high.' Another participant, who is currently looking for work, said they were worried there'd be less job vacancies because it'll be more expensive for companies to hire.	−2
R	N/A	0
S	This decision was extremely popular in the group. It was the policy most participants had heard of from the Budget without prompting. Several people said they'd already been researching how much money they'd be due to save in tax. 'Finally, the government is giving us a break,' said one man. 'Hats off to the chancellor.'	+4
T	This outcome and the way it had been reported in the media was the first point of discussion in the group, and there was unanimous criticism of you. Participants expressed strong disappointment that the government hadn't cut income tax when it had been a viable option pushed by the prime minister. There was also criticism of the apparent division at the top of the government. 'Can't sort themselves out, can they?' said one woman. 'They're all pulling in different directions. It's no way to run a country or the economy.'	−4

Add up the impacts of your policies on your approval rating. It's now time to check your popularity with the electorate. If your approval rating is less than zero, turn to Chapter 36 on p. 312. If your approval rating is zero or higher, turn to Chapter 37 on p. 317.

Democracy, Red in Tooth and Claw

FIVE WEEKS LATER

You're standing on a stage in your local village hall in the small hours of the morning, your stomach sick with nerves. It's been one of the closest general elections in recent history and the BBC's 10pm exit poll has the opposition on course for a narrow victory. You've been checking the early results coming in with Polly and they are indeed concerning. Key bellwether seats are being lost at an alarming rate. Next to be called is yours.

'The votes have been counted and I am now ready to announce the results for the constituency,' the returning officer says.

You're joined on stage by a colourful array of characters, including: the leader of the Monster Raving Loony Party; the local pub landlord who is standing as an independent; your chief constituency rival, Graham Taverner; a member of the 'England for the English' party; someone dressed as

Elmo from *Sesame Street*. A long line of TV cameras is filming this moment, correspondents standing by. The media know this could be one of the biggest moments of election night, an upset to rival Michael Portillo losing his seat at the 1997 general election. Taverner has a quietly confident look, adding to your nerves.

One of the reasons you're so worried is because you've had relatively little time to dedicate to your role as a constituency MP in between all the stresses and strains of being chancellor. That's left the field open for the likes of Graham Taverner – the man you beat to win this seat in the first place, who's bent on revenge – to pound the streets and knock on every door in the patch telling voters to kick you out and send a message to the government. The opposition also knows what a scalp it would be to unseat a sitting chancellor at an election, and hence they'd been piling resources into Taverner's campaign in the final weeks. Extra activists, extra placards, extra leaflets ... it's been an all-out assault. And going by the sizes of the stacks of ballot papers that you can see piled up on the counting tables next to Taverner's name compared to yours, you can tell this is going to be uncomfortably tight.

'Monster Raving Loony Party ... 94 votes!'

There is wild cheering at the back of the hall and the candidate pumps his fist.

'Graham Taverner ... 12,954 votes!'

The tally brings gasps of excitement. That's a lot of votes, more than you won at the last election. Taverner is nodding confidently. He thinks he's got enough.

'The candidate who wishes to be known as Elmo ... 12 votes!'

A singular female voice starts whooping madly and chants 'Elmo! Elmo! Elmo!' You look closer. It is in fact Polly. With your collective political careers in the balance, you're glad at least one of you is enjoying this moment.

Your name is read out next and you hold your breath. As you do, you have a consoling reflection: whatever happens next, you did your best. Running one of the world's largest economies is no easy feat and you've had to make many an unpopular decision. People like to snipe and armchair strategise from the sidelines, but you're the one who's had to make these momentous choices and live with the consequences. You know that you've always had the interests of the British people at heart, so come what may, you can hold your head up high. It feels like a long time before the returning officer speaks again.

'... 12,923 votes!'

There's a sudden roar of cheering and applause from Taverner's camp, mixed with seemingly thousands of camera flashes going off at once to capture your reaction. You do your best to mask your emotions and nod graciously, knowing this photo will feature in the history books. You are the first sitting chancellor to lose your seat at a general election.

Taverner makes his way to the podium for his victory speech. He says the public have sent a resounding message tonight that they're crying out for change, and that change begins now. He says he'll do everything to repay the people who've supported him, and everything to win over those who didn't.

'But let us be glad,' he says in closing. 'As we say goodbye to this wretched government!'

That brings more cheers from his supporters and you want nothing more than to get off that stage and away from the glare of those camera lights. A throng of reporters crowds you as you leave but you burst through and jump into a car with Polly heading straight back to London. You spend most of the journey in a melancholy silence, mulling over what went wrong. Could you have done more to win over the public? Did your Budget go far enough to show voters you were on their side? Did you ignore the vagaries of public opinion at your peril? These are the questions you'll be asking yourself for many years to come.

You return to Westminster and the removal vans are already parked up beside Downing Street by mid-morning, a sad and stark sight. The verdict of British democracy is as swift as it is brutal, and the business of government waits for no-one. One moment you're one of the most powerful people in the country. The next, you're nobody, just another unemployed citizen looking for a job. The press are already busy reporting on the new prime minister and their new government, seized by the excitement of a changing of the guard. You're now just an historical footnote.

As you pack away your final box of belongings and say goodbye to the Downing Street flat, you take a last look at the famous staircase of No. 11, with its portraits and cartoons of all the chancellors who've gone before you. Your face will soon appear on these walls and that's a source of personal pride. Not many people get to say they were the Chancellor of the Exchequer. But you can. And though the British people have delivered their verdict on your tenure in charge of the nation's finances – an unmistakable thumbs-down – you're proud to live in a country where the question of who governs is settled via the peaceful process of the ballot box. A phrase popularly attributed to Winston Churchill, one of your predecessors as chancellor, comes to mind as you leave

Downing Street for the last time: 'Democracy is the worst form of government, except for all those other forms that have been tried from time to time.'

Commiserations! Your time as chancellor has ended in defeat. Your stewardship of the economy wasn't enough to win over the public: you've lost your seat and the government has been voted from power.
Return to p. 153 to try again!

CHAPTER 37

A New Dawn Breaks

It's 2am and you're standing on a stage in your local village hall, about to learn your personal electoral fate. The polls closed four hours earlier on that great exercise in democracy – a general election – where the people of the UK momentarily seized control and cast their verdict on the powers that be, including yours truly. You're quietly optimistic: the BBC's exit poll has your party on course to win a narrow majority, and the early results of the night confirm that picture. The prime minister sent you a message just after the exit poll dropped – 'Mission accomplished?' – but you'd said to keep the champagne on ice. The night is still young.

'The ballots have been counted and I'm ready to announce the results,' your constituency's returning officer says.

The buzz in the hall grows. Alongside you is a line of rosette-bearing candidates, including: a member of the Monster Raving Loony Party; the popular pub landlord who is standing as an independent; a member of the 'England for the English' party; your closest rival, Graham Taverner; and also someone dressed as Elmo from *Sesame Street*. They're about to get their five seconds of fame as all the major news channels broadcast this moment live. The world is about to learn whether you, the Chancellor of the Exchequer, have retained your seat.

'Monster Raving Loony Party … 83 votes!'

There's a huge cheer at the back of the hall and the candidate raises his fist triumphantly. You're aware that all the TV cameras are trained on you.

'Graham Taverner … 12,831 votes!'

Ooos of intrigue fill the hall. Now you're feeling worried because that's a lot of votes, more than you won at the last election. One of the disadvantages of being chancellor is that you have less time to commit to your local constituency, so while you've been off at international summits and preparing Budgets, your local rival Graham has been working his socks off campaigning and urging everyone in your area to kick you out and give the government a bloody nose. You and Graham have history – he's the guy you defeated to originally win this seat, and no doubt he wants his revenge – and you see his smirk out of the side of your eye. But there's no time to dwell further because the results keep coming.

'The candidate who wishes to be known as Elmo … 12 votes!'

A singular female voice starts whooping wildly at the back of the hall and chants 'Elmo! Elmo! Elmo!' You take a closer look. It is in fact Polly. She gives you a big double thumbs-up. Your name is read out next, and a sudden hush falls over the hall.

In those moments of silence before the returning officer announces your result, you have a consoling thought: you tried your best. You were charged with running one of the world's largest economies and you bore the burden of power to the best of your ability. Were mistakes made? Undoubtedly. But to govern is to choose, and you always chose in good faith, with the interests of the British people at heart. So, whatever happens next, you can hold your head high.

'... 12,923 votes!'

Elation washes over you. Your team are clapping and cheering and Polly is celebrating like she's just won the World Cup. You give a measured smile for the cameras but retain your composure while the rest of the votes are announced. Then you take to the podium for your victory speech. You thank the returning officer and everyone involved for the smooth running of the election, and congratulate your opponents on a race well run. You reflect on how lucky we all are to live in a democracy where the question of the exercise of power is settled peacefully, with pencils marking crosses on paper ballots in polling stations across the country, instead of through violence, intimidation or coercion. You conclude by saying it's the privilege of your life to serve your constituents, and you will continue to do so with all your heart.

Polly gives you a big hug in the backseat of the car as you head back to London and says she's got even more good news. On a night where your party continues to rack up wins across the country and you edge closer to the magic number for a parliamentary majority, someone dear to you has also secured their place on the famous green benches, a last-minute replacement in a hotly contested constituency where the incumbent MP had to withdraw shortly before the election due to ill health.

'She's only gone and done it ...' Polly says. 'June won her seat!'

Cue more hugs. The celebratory mood continues despite your sleep deprivation as you return to party HQ in Westminster, where you find your exhausted campaign staff running on adrenaline and the thrill of sweet impending victory. The following hours involve a montage of moments that will be marked in the history books: the prime minister's 5am victory speech, her visit to the Palace to see the king, her remarks to the nation on the steps of 10 Downing Street with the morning light breaking. You're the first person to be invited to join her in the Cabinet room as she appoints her government, and you share a long and warm embrace. Any disagreements, arguments, misunderstandings, squabbles or enmity that might have passed between you, it all feels forgotten now amid the warm glow of outright triumph. Emily asks if you would do her the honour of serving as her chancellor, and you accept.

'What did I say?' she says, eyes glistening. 'Never in doubt. Five more years.'

The Cabinet appointments continue through the afternoon, during which time you take a much-needed nap in the No. 11 flat, feeling very glad that you don't need to call in the removal vans. You wake in the early evening and take a moment to step out into Downing Street, drinking in the occasion and everything you've achieved. Just hours earlier, the prime minister was stood on the very spot where you are now, addressing the nation and setting out her hopes and ambitions for the years ahead. You turn to face the famous black door of No. 10 and hear the echo of a half-remembered phrase, something Polly had said on the day when you were first appointed chancellor. What were her words? They come back to you now. *A stone's throw away …*

Congratulations! You have succeeded in your journey as chancellor. You have steered the economy through troubled times and helped your party win a general election. Your name will go down in political and economic history. Well done!

Throughout your journey you've received advice and wisdom from chancellors who've gone before you. To read more about their experiences from interviews with the author, continue to p. 323.

APPENDICES

The Chancellors

NORMAN LAMONT

Norman Lamont was Chancellor of the Exchequer from 28 November 1990 to 27 May 1993. The first person to hold all three positions of Financial Secretary to the Treasury (often known as the City minister), Chief Secretary to the Treasury and then chancellor, Lamont was appointed to the role by Prime Minister John Major, having previously served in the Cabinet of Margaret Thatcher. Lamont took over the Treasury at a time of high inflation and with the economy in recession. Governing in a period when interest rates were still decided by the government rather than the Bank of England, an important feature of Lamont's tenure was Britain's membership of the European Exchange Rate Mechanism (ERM), a commitment to peg the value of sterling to the German currency, the Deutschmark, in a bid to curb inflation. Lamont was famously at the helm when Britain withdrew from the ERM in 1992 on what became known as

Black Wednesday. He then changed the UK's monetary policy framework to target inflation within a range of 1–4 per cent, an innovation which ultimately led to the 2 per cent inflation target that persists today.

'I had an immense crisis,' Lamont said of the Black Wednesday episode, when the government increased interest rates and the BOE spent billions of pounds to prop up the value of sterling to remain within the ERM, before eventually letting the pound devalue. 'Or, it was thought to be an immense crisis. I think historically it may look like less of a crisis than it did at the time. It taught me that one always has to be very careful about the markets. The ERM crisis showed that the firepower of the markets was far greater than the firepower of central banks, even central banks acting in coordination and cooperation.'

Lamont said the Black Wednesday episode led to him becoming the most unpopular man in Britain, fulfilling a prediction that had been made to him by the Treasury when he first arrived in the role. Nevertheless, according to Lamont, being able to endure unpopularity is an important part of the role of chancellor.

'One of the functions of a politician is to take public criticism, to take abuse,' Lamont said. 'The way we maintain stability in a democracy is people having someone to blame, a scapegoat, someone at whom they can throw a rotten tomato.' Lamont cited a quotation from the conservative statesman and philosopher Edmund Burke: 'Obloquy is a necessary ingredient in the composition of all true glory.' 'I think there's something in that,' Lamont said.

According to Lamont, this stoic attitude to public criticism also extends to how the chancellor should consider media coverage.

'It's very important as chancellor not to pay too much attention to what the tabloids write about short-term decisions,' Lamont said. 'You should take a longer-term view. Public opinion, and even tabloid newspapers, surprisingly often alter their opinion.'

Unlike the modern practice of Budget policies being extensively trailed in the media, Lamont said he tried his utmost to preserve the secrecy of all of his measures.

'We kept things under wraps,' Lamont said. 'We did not leak. But journalists being journalists, they did try very hard to discover the Budget's contents, or they might float things. It was quite funny really: before Budgets, one would see a whole lot of forecasts, speculation about this might happen, that. And one would notice the one report that was true or accurate and wonder whether it was a leak, or it may not have been a leak at all.'

Lamont said one of the trickiest aspects of being chancellor is managing relations with your fellow Cabinet colleagues, and particularly the prime minister, who have less of a focus on making the sums add up.

'The Treasury is the only department that is wanting to balance the Budget, balance the books, to make sure that the country does not become indebted,' he said. 'Every person around the Cabinet table has got their own pet project where they just feel a little bit of flexibility, a little bit of imagination, they will all endlessly say "it pays for itself", "the narrow minded view of the Treasury is not to take these things into account", blah, blah, blah. The chancellor can only get the Cabinet to be responsible if he has the backing of the prime minister.'

The issue is complicated by the prime minister's official status as 'First Lord of the Treasury', which Lamont believes Mrs Thatcher was keenly aware of.

'Although the prime minister can see that it's important to support the chancellor, the prime minister is also like everyone else around the Cabinet table, a politician worried about getting re-elected,' he said. 'So the prime minister may be supporting the chancellor, but they will also have some sympathy with the things being said around the Cabinet table.'

Lamont delivered three Budgets: in 1991, 1992 and 1993. His '91 Budget included a reduction in the infamous poll tax, while his '92 Budget introduced a 20p rate of income tax on the first £2,000 of earnings. His Budget in '93, among other measures, raised VAT on energy bills and froze income tax thresholds, effectively amounting to tax rises.

'One was thought of as a horror show [the 1993 Budget],' he said. 'One was very well received [the 1991 Budget]. The middle one [in 1992] I think was just plain boring. It was quite a worthy Budget. I remember thinking as I delivered it, "Hmm, is this very interesting?"'

Lamont said he's nevertheless not sure if the spectacle of a Budget is the best way to manage the country's finances.

'It's rather odd that we in this country have an annual Budget,' he said. 'It's not quite Derby Day, but there's a degree of festivity. Other countries don't have this drama. They make these changes in tax and expenditure on a rolling, continuous basis. Some of the drama could be taken out of it, probably with quite good effect.'

PHILIP HAMMOND

Philip Hammond was Chancellor of the Exchequer from 13 July 2016 to 24 July 2019. Appointed by new prime minister Theresa May – the successor to David Cameron, who had

resigned after Britain voted to quit the European Union –
Hammond's chancellorship was dominated by the question
of Brexit and how the UK would go about splitting from the
EU, its largest trading partner. Hammond took the reins as
chancellor from George Osborne, who'd run the Treasury
since 2010 and had sought to repair Britain's public finances
after the global financial crisis. Hammond said he had two
objectives when he became chancellor: protecting the economy against damage from Brexit and continuing the process
of stabilising the public finances.

'My focus was sustaining growth at a time when I thought
the economy was very vulnerable because of Brexit,' he said.
'We didn't know what Brexit was going to look like.'

Because of his focus on growth and the lack of an imminent election – the next national vote wasn't due until 2020
– Hammond said he felt relatively insulated from electoral
and media pressure as chancellor. He said his aim was to be
seen as a competent chancellor, not a popular one.

'I was always much more interested in the business and
markets' reaction than the *Daily Mail* reaction,' he said. 'I
probably had a 100:1 weighting. If I got 10 good business
comments, no end of pages of the *Daily Mail* and the *Sun*
criticising bothered me. When you should start to worry is
when the popular rags and the business community and the
markets are giving you the thumbs-down at the same time.'

Hammond delivered three Budgets. The first, in March
2017, included a controversial decision to increase National
Insurance contributions for self-employed people, a policy
which was a breach of the Conservative Party's 2015 mani-
festo pledge not to increase National Insurance. Hammond
had to U-turn on the measure after a strong backlash, including from many of his own MPs. His November 2017 Budget

included measures to support home ownership, including abolishing stamp duty on first-time buyer purchases up to £300,000. His third and final Budget, in October 2018, delivered tax cuts in the form of raising the thresholds at which people start to pay the basic and higher rates of income tax.

Hammond said he had a strong preference for working from No. 11 rather than the Treasury when he was chancellor, especially due to the intensity of the post-Brexit vote political intrigue that gripped Westminster.

'The action was in Downing Street,' he said. 'I needed to keep an eye on what was going on. I needed to be physically close. My office was 40 yards from Gavin Barwell [Theresa May's chief of staff]'s office. I would be sending my people scuttling backwards and forwards all day long. The whole Brexit thing was totally dominating the agenda.'

At the end of Hammond's tenure as chancellor, the UK's debt to GDP ratio – a key measure of the country's indebtedness – was about 84 per cent. As of 2025, it had risen to almost 100 per cent, in large part due to significant extra government borrowing to fund support for the public during the coronavirus pandemic of 2020–1. Hammond said the UK's vulnerable financial position means the government would have limited options if another major crisis struck.

'We're now at a place where I don't think we've got very much fiscal headroom,' he said. 'If another major crisis struck, I don't think we'd be able to run up extra hundreds of billions of public borrowing in the way we did during Covid.'

Hammond said the Budget is a privilege for the chancellor and the biggest political set-piece of the year, bigger than any parliamentary moment enjoyed by the prime minister. He said it's important to have a crowd-pleasing announcement in the final paragraphs of the speech – the rabbit from the hat, so to speak – and also to have a few jokes.

'The jokes exercised me enormously,' he said. 'The night before the Budget I would be typically up until one or two in the morning trying to get the final jokes to work.'

KWASI KWARTENG

Kwasi Kwarteng was Chancellor of the Exchequer from 6 September 2022 to 14 October 2022. His 38-day tenure was the second shortest in the history of the role, beaten only by Iain Macleod in 1970, who died after a month. Appointed by Liz Truss – who had just become prime minister after winning the Conservative Party's leadership election following the resignation of Boris Johnson – Kwarteng delivered a single fiscal event on 23 September 2022. Named 'The Growth Plan', and widely dubbed a 'mini-Budget', the package included cutting the basic rate of income tax from 20 per cent to 19 per cent, abolishing the 45 per cent higher rate of income tax, cancelling a planned increase in corporation tax, cutting the National Insurance payroll tax and freezing energy bills. It was the biggest set of tax cuts in 50 years.

The measures, which were announced without an accompanying OBR analysis or forecast, triggered a significant backlash on financial markets as investors balked at the scale of the unfunded commitments. The pound crashed and the government's borrowing costs soared, prompting an emergency intervention by the Bank of England. Lenders pulled more than 40 per cent of mortgage products amid the market turmoil, with the cost of a five-year fixed-rate mortgage breaching 6 per cent for the first time in more than a decade.

In response, Kwarteng defended the mini-Budget, though the government did reverse the abolition of the 45 per cent income tax rate. On 12 October 2022, Kwarteng travelled to Washington for the IMF's annual meetings. However, he cut the trip short and returned to London on 14 October 2022, where he was sacked by Truss. Truss herself resigned six days later.

Kwarteng said his experience illustrated the power of the OBR and the importance of presenting financial plans that are fully costed.

'The kind of dramatic tax cuts we brought about needed to be funded, probably through reductions in spending,' he said. 'But that was something we were unwilling to countenance. There weren't any spending cuts in my statement. That was one of the principal errors that was made.'

According to Kwarteng, the decision to bypass the OBR at the mini-Budget came from a view that the body had only been around for about ten years, so it could be ignored.

'But it had rapidly become a kind of totem for the market,' he said. 'You couldn't get around it. You've got to work with them.'

The other major error at the mini-Budget was moving too quickly, and Kwarteng feels the pressure to do so came from the prime minister.

'What you can't do is just rush in and try and do everything at once,' he said. 'That was really what brought Truss down. It was the pace with which she wanted to move, and not being able to prepare the ground over a longer period of time, to land the strategy of what you're trying to do.'

Kwarteng said he'd nevertheless wanted to defend the government's position for longer, and that the chancellor ought to try to stay above the fray of daily financial market movements and media commentary. (Kwarteng said he didn't read the newspapers.) However, matters were taken out of his hands by No. 10.

'No. 10 capitulated very quickly,' he said. 'All I remember from my brief time in Downing Street was chaos and panic, really.'

Kwarteng described his trip to Washington and eventual sacking as an 'extraordinary' episode which hastened Truss's demise.

'I knew the government was under intense pressure and the polls had collapsed,' he said. 'But I didn't see how removing me would improve the situation. In fact, I think it made it worse for the prime minister. It meant she had very little road left. As soon as you get rid of the chancellor, the new chancellor suddenly becomes the most powerful person in the government. Because the prime minister is weakened because their first choice has been sacked. And the second person is unsackable. As soon as [Jeremy] Hunt took over, the civil service guys were saying, "He's the prime minister in reality." When I went away to Washington, she was advised to sack me, or to try and reverse course. In the end, the prime minister just blew up. I was quite relieved to leave Downing Street, frankly.'

JEREMY HUNT

Jeremy Hunt was Chancellor of the Exchequer from 14 October 2022 to 5 July 2024. Appointed at a moment of crisis – Liz Truss's Conservative administration was still reeling from the market backlash to the government's tax-cutting mini-Budget and Kwasi Kwarteng had just been fired – he remembers the sense of excitement and apprehension as he was met on the Treasury's steps by James Bowler, the department's permanent secretary.

'The Treasury's reputation was on the line,' he said. 'We had a £72 billion black hole. They must have been thinking: is this guy willing to take the difficult decisions we've now got to take? It was a big moment.'

His first act as chancellor was to reverse most of the tax-cutting mini-Budget, a move that stabilised the government's financial position. Truss resigned three days later and was succeeded as prime minister by Rishi Sunak, who reappointed Hunt as chancellor. Hunt then delivered the first of his four fiscal events with an Autumn Statement on 17 November 2022. Facing high levels of inflation due to the energy crisis sparked by Russia's war in Ukraine and against the backdrop of predictions of a lengthy recession, Hunt announced a package of tax hikes and spending cuts to repair the public finances, while also offering help with the cost of living. His Spring Budget on 15 March 2023 focused on growing the economy by getting more people into work, before his Autumn Statement on 22 November 2023 and Spring Budget on 6 March 2024 both delivered cuts to national insurance rates for employees as the Conservatives looked to win public support ahead of the 2024 general election. Hunt also introduced a major corporate tax break called full expensing, allowing companies to deduct the cost of investments in plant and machinery from their tax bills, in a bid to spur economic growth by encouraging improvements in productivity.

'I always had a rule in every Budget or Autumn Statement that I wanted to do one really big thing that stood the test of time, so people would look back on that event and say, "That was a really good Budget,"' Hunt said. 'All of those reforms have stayed. But it took a lot of work and thinking to get them into place.'

Hunt said one of his scariest moments as chancellor was when his March '23 Budget almost unravelled over his decision to scrap the annual limit on how much people could save tax-free in their pensions, a move intended to encourage older people back into work but attacked by then-shadow Labour chancellor Rachel Reeves as a 'free-for-all for the wealthy few'.

'Because of Kwasi Kwarteng's budget completely unravelling six months earlier, Labour were smelling blood,' he said. 'They were thinking they could get this Budget to unravel as well.'

However, to Hunt's great surprise given his clashes with this body during his previous tenure as health secretary, the British Medical Association (BMA) announced its fulsome support for the plan shortly before Hunt's crunch post-Budget interview on the *Today* programme. The BMA said that senior doctors were already indicating they'd be returning to work because of the policy.

'I knew then I was going to be alright,' Hunt said. 'But there was a moment where I wasn't quite sure which way it was going to go.'

Hunt said the hardest thing about being chancellor is prioritising the long term. He said the common thinking is that being chancellor is about making trade-offs – such as whether to fund the NHS or defence, or whether to build this bridge or that nuclear power plant – but the real trade-off is between the short term and the long term.

'There are so many things putting pressure on you to be short-term,' he said. 'The politics before an election. You've got all these MPs saying, "If this bridge isn't built in my constituency, I'm going to lose the election.' You've got No. 10, not just the prime minister but his team, who are very political. The hardest thing is locking down long-term reforms.'

According to Hunt, the best thing about being chancellor is how much you can achieve in a short period of time. Despite more than a decade in the Cabinet – serving in roles including culture secretary, health secretary and foreign secretary – Hunt said he got more done as chancellor in two years than he did in all those other government roles.

'I can point to one or two big things that I did that I'm proud of in all the roles I did,' he said, citing examples like his work on the 2012 Olympics, reducing baby deaths in the NHS and laying the groundwork for the freeing of Nazanin Zagari-Radcliffe. 'As chancellor, I did 14 things I really wanted to do for a very long time. I was so long in the tooth that I really knew what I wanted to do. It was like being a boy in a sweet shop.'

Being chancellor was also a source of significant personal pride. Hunt's brother died of cancer during his chancellorship, but he was able to watch Hunt deliver the March '23 Budget from the gallery of the House of Commons.

'He didn't have any hair because of his chemotherapy,' Hunt said. 'It meant a lot to me. That's something that you remember.'

Hunt said the Treasury has an understandable institutional focus on making the sums add up for the Budget, because it's the chancellor's biggest event of the year, but that such a focus on tax and spending can come at the expense of doing work focused on boosting productivity and working to grow the economy. He also said his biggest failure was not doing enough to convey optimism and hope for the British economy, which is a key responsibility for the chancellor.

'You are salesman-in-chief,' he said. 'Don't forget the communications.'

RACHEL REEVES

Rachel Reeves was appointed Chancellor by Prime Minister Keir Starmer on 5 July 2024 following Labour's general election victory, becoming the first woman to hold the role in its more-than-800-year history. One of her first acts as chancellor was to commission an audit of Treasury spending, which found £22 billion of unfunded commitments. She responded by cutting back various policies, such as new road and railway schemes, and by axing winter fuel payments for wealthier pensioners. Reeves was criticised at the time for painting an overly pessimistic picture of the UK's economic position, which coincided with a slump in consumer confidence and weakening growth.

Reeves gave her first Budget on 30 October 2024. It included £40 billion of tax increases to fund more spending on the NHS and public services, while also loosening the government's fiscal rules around borrowing to allow for more capital investment. Under the plans she'd inherited from Hunt, capital spending, which covers outlays such as building new schools, roads and hospitals, was due to decline from 2.5 per cent of GDP in 2023–4 to 1.7 per cent of GDP in 2028–9. Reeves said her Budget decisions were necessary to put the country's finances on a firm footing, while also creating the conditions for future economic growth.

'We stabilised the situation,' she said. 'It was really important for rebuilding the foundations of the country.'

Reeves said her top priority as chancellor is raising the UK's growth rate. Britain's economy has grown more slowly than the US, the Eurozone average and Japan's since the coronavirus pandemic, an issue Reeves wants to address.

'The best thing for fiscal sustainability is a healthy, growing economy that sees debt fall as a share of GDP, not just because you're addressing the numerator, debt, but because you're addressing the denominator, GDP,' she said. 'That is how, in the past, we've had sustainable public finances.'

Every weekend, Reeves said she runs through a growth tracker, which contains about a hundred different projects the government wants to happen to boost growth. Then she and her team spend the week working with other government departments to unlock those projects.

Reeves said her decision to move to one major fiscal event a year – a Budget in the autumn, and aiming to have no significant tax or spending changes at the Spring Statement – is also partly to encourage more of a focus in the Treasury on economic growth and the drivers of growth, rather than spending too much time on tax, spending and the fiscal position.

'I spend as much time in the department on meetings around growth and designing growth policies as designing fiscal policy,' she said. 'I don't think the balance has been right in the last few years where it's just moving from fiscal event to fiscal event.'

Nevertheless, Reeves did have to announce significant changes to her spending plans at her first Spring Statement on 26 March 2025. After a rise in government borrowing costs since her first Budget, largely driven by higher interest rate expectations due to the expected tariff policies of US President Donald Trump, and amid weaker projections for the UK economy, Reeves was told by the OBR that she was on course to miss her key fiscal rule by £4 billion. Reeves responded by cutting welfare and the overall level of public spending, restoring her fiscal buffer to about £10 billion.

Reeves said it's crucial to have strong fiscal rules and that they help the chancellor manage the political pressures of the role.

'You've got to have some sort of anchor for fiscal policy,' she said. 'You've got a binding constraint on what you can do on the tax and spending side, and you've got to make sure that adds up at all times. You can't say yes to everything. The prime minister knows that. The Cabinet knows that. It does give you a sort of backstop. That's not unhelpful for a chancellor.'

Becoming the first female chancellor was a proud moment for Reeves. She remembers the applause that broke out in the Treasury during her first speech to staff when she mentioned the fact.

'That was really lovely,' she said. 'There are people who've worked there, in some cases from the 1990s, and they've worked under a lot of different chancellors, but that's a massive thing in their careers to have a woman doing this job. I'm very proud of that. But there's also a big responsibility to show that a woman can do the job.'

Author's Note

Aside from named historical figures and chancellors, the characters in this book are fictional and not a representation of real people.

Tax rates referenced in this book are accurate as of September 2025. They may, of course, change at future Budgets. Calculations about the revenue impact of tax changes were made using the January 2025 edition of the Treasury's 'Direct effects of illustrative tax changes bulletin'.

The statistics concerning the size of government revenue and spending in Chapter 2, public sector pay in Chapter 3, and the approximate cost of the pensions triple lock in Chapter 16, were taken from the Institute for Fiscal Studies. Net-migration figures in Chapter 8 are from the Office for National Statistics' 'Long-term international migration, provisional: year ending June 2024'. The estimated £4 billion cost of a £20 weekly increase in Universal Credit in Chapter 27 is taken from a Policy in Practice report ('Uprating Universal Credit to tackle the cost of living crisis') to the Centre for Social Justice in 2022.

The quotations at the start of chapters from Norman Lamont, Philip Hammond, Kwasi Kwarteng, Jeremy Hunt and Rachel Reeves are taken from original interviews conducted by the author in spring 2025. The quotations from

James Callaghan, Roy Jenkins, Denis Healey, Alistair Darling and Gordon Brown come from their respective memoirs:

> James Callaghan, *Time and Chance* (William Collins Sons & Co. Ltd, 1987), pp. 180, 193
> Roy Jenkins, *A Life at the Centre* (Methuen Publishing Ltd, 2006), pp. 231, 245
> Denis Healey, *The Time of My Life* (Penguin, 1989), pp. 377, 383, 388
> Gordon Brown, *My Life, Our Times* (Vintage, 2017), p. 127
> Alistair Darling, *Back from the Brink* (Atlantic Books, 2012), pp. 18, 225

In Chapter 14, you are given the option of signing a comprehensive free-trade agreement with the United States. Note, the UK and US announced an economic accord in May 2025 that was billed as a 'major trade deal' by President Donald Trump. In fact, the agreement fell far short of a full FTA. The accord reduced some of the tariffs that had been levied on Britain by Trump's administration, particularly facing carmakers.

Throughout the book, I sought to present choices that reflect those currently facing the Treasury. Chapter 16 is an exception, where it's assumed that the government has already dropped the 'triple lock' commitment on the state pension. At the time of publication, the triple lock remains in place, though its future is perennially a point of speculation.

In Chapter 24, you have the option of imposing a one-off wealth tax. The expected revenue gains from the policy are taken from a report ('A wealth tax for the UK') by the Wealth Tax Commission published in 2020.

You started your journey with a surplus of £20 billion. For context, this is less than the near £30 billion of headroom that chancellors have averaged against their fiscal rules since 2010, but it's more than the £8.9 billion of headroom that Rachel Reeves inherited from Jeremy Hunt in 2024. If you found it tricky to keep the public finances in the black throughout this book, you might have some sympathy with our recent chancellors who've had to operate with even less.

UK fiscal margin against current mandate

■ Osborne (Coalition) ■ Osborne ■ Hammond ■ Sunak ▨ Hunt ▨ Reeves

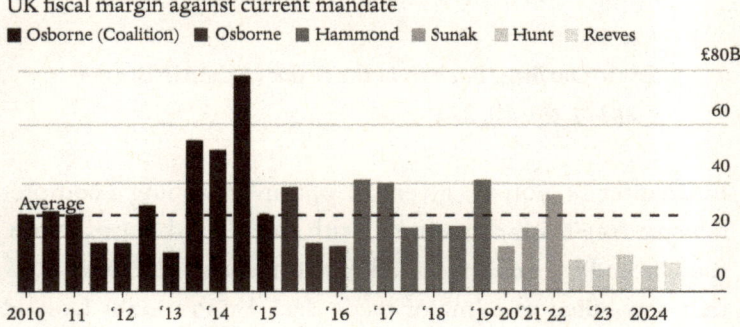

Source: Office for Budget Responsibility, HM Treasury

YOUR BUDGET SCORECARD

Policy Area	Option	Cost / Revenue

Total cost / revenue of Budget measures	
Starting surplus / deficit	
Final Budget position	

YOUR BUDGET SCORECARD

Policy Area	Option	Cost / Revenue

Total cost / revenue of Budget measures	
Starting surplus / deficit	
Final Budget position	

OFFICIAL – SENSITIVE